Practical Sewing and Dressmaking

PRACTICAL SEWING AND DRESSMAKING

Practical
Sewing and Dressmaking

BY

SARA MAY ALLINGTON

ILLUSTRATED BY

ELIZABETH CLEVES BANKS

BOSTON
DANA ESTES & COMPANY
PUBLISHERS

THE COLONIAL PRESS
C. H. SIMONDS & CO., BOSTON, U. S A.

7

CONTENTS

CONTENTS

CONTENTS

CONTENTS

INTRODUCTION

EVERY woman, no matter how she may be situated at the present time, should have at her command some knowledge which, if circumstances demand it suddenly, would bring her in a good income.

There is no business in the world, for which women are fitted, which brings in a greater income for so little expenditure of capital and time as dressmaking

There is no woman who will not wish some time in her life that she knew something of this art. If she has children she will wish to make many things for them. If she is not a woman of wealth, she can dress herself for less than half what it will cost her to hire, if she can make her own clothing Even should she be able to hire her work done, if she understands the work herself, how much easier it is for her to be suited with the work of others. There are none so hard to please as those who do not know how a thing should be done

Oftentimes a financial crisis comes suddenly into one's life, when there is no time to wait for positions and hardly time to think what to do With the knowledge of sewing and dressmaking, one can turn to it and earn a good income, at almost a moment's notice.

Almost every day we hear of women who are thrown out into the world to earn their own living. With the thorough knowledge of sewing and dressmaking we have tried to give in these pages, she can make a success wherever she may wish to put her knowledge to the test.

In almost any line of work the competition is so great that it is difficult to find a position, and in almost every line the woman is forced to work in competition with men, under the nervous strain of business methods and at much smaller pay than that of the man working beside her. This is not so with sewing and dressmaking. The field is hers, and it is so large that there is still room for many more workers.

We have tried to give in this course a method so simple and a course so thorough and broad that it will meet the needs of all women, no matter for what purpose they may wish to use their knowledge.

PRACTICAL SEWING AND DRESSMAKING

LESSON I

STITCHES USED IN DRESSMAKING AND SEWING

BEFORE taking up the actual making of the gown, we will learn the different stitches and utensils which are necessary for dressmaking and sewing.

Basting. — For basting use a good quality basting thread. No. 60 is preferable for all uses except very heavy wool goods, then it is best to use 40 or 50. For silk or velvet a fine thread should be used so that it will not mark the goods. In pulling out bastings never try to pull the entire length of the thread. Cut it every few stitches or you will pull the thread in the goods and ruin it.

Even Basting is where the stitch is the same length on both sides. This is used for basting up seams.

Uneven Basting is where the upper stitch is long and the under one short. It is used for marking seams, basting in hems, etc.

Slanting or Padding Stitch is used for fastening in canvas or padding in coats.

Running Stitch is where small stitches are taken evenly. This is used for joining pieces of materials, tucks, gathers, and sewing on braid or trimming   The work should be held evenly together with the left hand, while the needle is held in the right and pushed back and forth through the material, making as many stitches on the needle as possible before pulling it through. You should practice this stitch until you can take small even stitches without looking at the work.

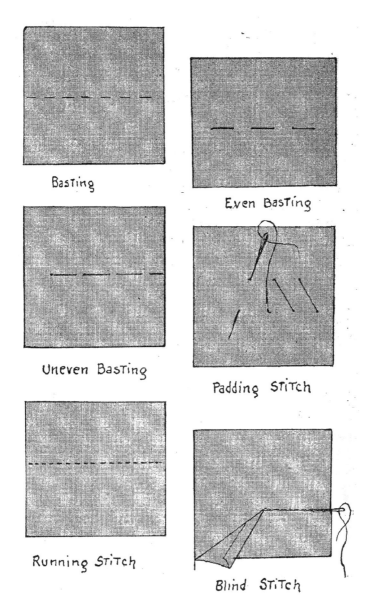

Basting

Even Basting

Uneven Basting

Padding Stitch

Running Stitch

Blind Stitch

Blind Stitch. — This is used to fasten on trimming or bias bands where the stitch must not show on the right side. Run the needle between the foundation goods and the trimming with a running stitch. Take the stitch through the foundation, but only through the under side of the trimming or into the turned in edge of the bias band.

Back Stitch. — Make a stitch as in the running stitch. Instead of taking the next stitch beyond the first, place the needle way back in the next stitch and take one twice as long. Take each one way back to the one preceding it. This stitch is used to take the place of machine sewing. It is much stronger than the running stitch. When finished it should resemble machine stitching.

Overcasting is a slanting stitch taken over and over the raw edge of the goods. This is used on seams or wherever there is a raw edge exposed, to keep it from raveling. The work is done from right to left.

Overhanding. — The two selvages of goods are held evenly together and are sewed over and over together with very small slanting stitches. Where two raw edges are to be sewed together, the raw edges should be turned down a small seam and the edges thus formed held together the same as if they were selvages. The stitches should be very small and even. The work is done from right to left.

Hemming. — The hem is used to finish the edge and is turned down twice. The first turn is always as narrow as possible, and the second whatever width the hem is to be when finished. If the hem is to be put in on the machine it can be done with the foot attachment, unless too wide, but if it is to be hand work, it must always be basted. Take the stitch first in the cloth, then in the edge of the hem, and so on, making the stitches slanting and as small as possible. The stitch which is taken in the cloth should only take up one or two threads, so that it will not show on the right side. On skirts where the hem is too full to turn up, a piece of the goods cut just the same curve of the skirt and the

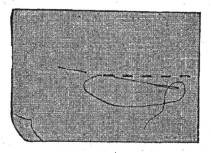

Back Stitch

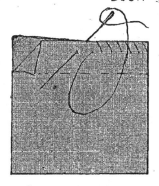

Over casting

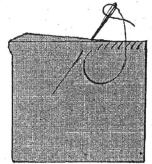

Over Handing

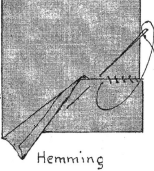

Hemming

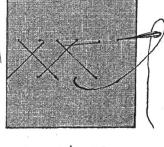

Cat Stitching

same way of the cloth is sewed to the bottom of the skirt, having the facing the width the hem is to be and on the right side of the skirt. Stitch and turn on the wrong side and fasten in place.

Cat-stitching. — This is used where the goods is too heavy to turn in twice. Turn the hem up the desired width without having turned in the edge. Hold the work so that the hem will run away from you Take a stitch first in the hem and then in the goods, in the hem again and again in the goods, holding the point of the needle towards you and making the stitches cross each other so that they resemble a rail fence.

French Knots. — These are little knots used for decorative purposes. Put the needle up through the goods from the wrong side Before pulling it through the goods, wind the thread about it three or four times. Hold the thread down to the needle with the left thumb. Put the needle down through as near the same place where it came up as possible. Draw down so that the knot looks smooth.

Button-holes. — Button-holes should always be cut very evenly They should be a little longer than the diameter of the button. It is a good plan to use button-hole scissors for cutting them More than one thickness of goods should be used and it should be firmly basted together If the material frays easily, it is a good plan to stitch around the button-hole before it is cut Button-holes should always be stayed before they are worked. One way is to overcast the button-hole. Another is to form stitches about the button-hole. Put the needle through from the under side, a few threads from the inside end of the button-hole Draw it through. Put it through again at the outside end of the button-hole very near the end and so the long stitch thus formed will lie close along the side of the button-hole. Repeat this a second time. This will form a bar of stitches about the button-hole When it is worked, begin at the right end and work towards the left To make the button-hole stitch, put the needle up through the goods a few threads from the inner end

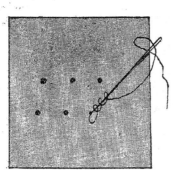
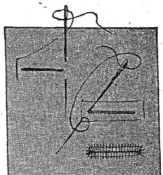

French Knots   BoTTon Hole

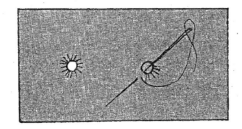

EyeleTS

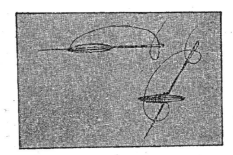

Loop

of the button-hole. Before pulling it through, take hold of the thread near the needle, throw it over the needle and pull through. Repeat this for each stitch until you have been around the button-hole. The beauty of the button-hole is to have the stitches all one length and perfectly even

To Work Button-holes on Lace. — Place a piece of thin goods underneath where the button-hole is to be worked. Baste into place. Cut the button-hole through the lace and goods. After it has been worked, cut away the goods so that it will not show.

Eyelets are small round holes punched in the goods with a stiletto and worked around over and over They are used largely on shirt-waists, where one wishes to put buttons through the goods so they can be easily removed

Loops. — Take three or four stitches about ¼ of an inch long on top of each other. Button-hole-stitch them all together, covering the entire length. This makes a strong loop which is used to take the place of the metal eye where the metal would show.

Finishing Seams. — Seams are finished in various ways. The plain seam is simply stitched up and pressed open, after each side has been thoroughly overcast.

Double Stitch Seam is stitched the same as the plain seam. Instead of pressing it open, press it all one way and stitch on the outside about ¼ of an inch from the first stitching.

French Seam. — Stitch the seam on the right side. Trim off close to the stitching. Turn and stitch on the wrong side The last stitching should come just where the seam in the garment should be

Strap Seam. — Make a bias band of the goods, turning in each edge The band should be on a true bias. Stitch the seam up on the right side, press open and place the bias band over it. Baste carefully and stitch very near each edge. This is used on coats, coat suits and skirts It makes a very neat trimming. The bias band may be used any desired width.

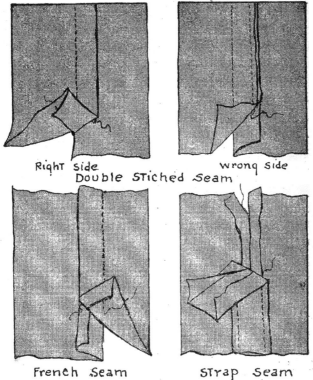

Right Side   wrong side
Double Stiched Seam

French Seam   Strap Seam

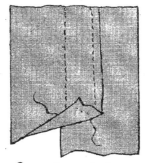

Raw Lap seam

Raw Lapped Seam. — Place one edge of the goods flat on the other and stitch very near each raw edge. This is good for very heavy wool goods.

Cord Seam. — Cover a small cord with the goods. Turn in one side of the seam and baste the cord along the seam. Lay flat on the other side of the seam and stitch on the right side very near the cord.

Fell Seam. — Stitch the seam as for a plain seam. Turn both edges one way Trim off the under edge quite narrow. Turn in the raw edge of the one not trimmed and stitch down flat, stitching as near the edge as possible.

Bias Bands. — To cut bias bands, fold the corner of the goods up so that the two straight edges of the triangle are the same length. Make a crease. Measure off the width the bands are to be and draw lines with a yardstick and tailors' chalk. Mark off as many bands as needed before cutting. Cut on the marks carefully, as the least change will throw the bands off the true bias. Bias bands of thin material, like silk, should be made over crinoline before being used

Milliners' Fold. — This is used as a trimming Make a bias band. Turn down one edge about $\frac{1}{2}$ the width of the band. Turn down the other about $\frac{1}{4}$ of an inch. Turn the narrow edge half way up on the broad edge and blind stitch

Girdles. — A girdle should always be made on linen canvas. It may be cut by a pattern to fit, or cut on a true bias and stretched to the figure. The goods may be put on full, plain, or in even folds, just as the style demands. The girdle should be boned to hold up stiff and smooth

Shirring. — Shirring may be done in two ways·

Plain Shirring. — Run the thread through the goods with very small and even stitches. Push the goods up on the thread until it is the desired fullness Be careful not to get it too full or it will lose its beauty Put in as many threads as you wish, at an equal distance apart. Put all the threads in before shoving the goods up, and keep the fullness the same on each thread

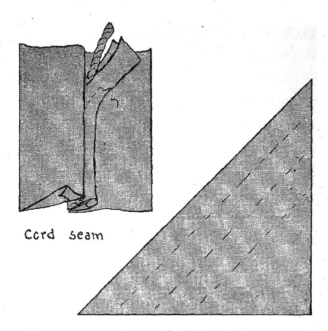

Cord seam

Bias Bands

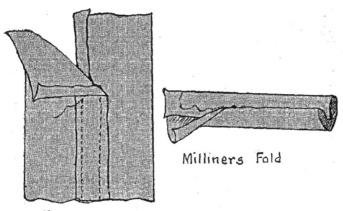

Fell seam

Milliners Fold

Tuck Shirring. — Instead of just running the thread in, as in plain shirring, take up a tuck each time about 1-8 of an inch wide   Shove up on the thread the same as in plain shirring Make as many tucks as desired, equally distant from each other.

LESSON II

FOR your work in sewing and dressmaking you will need a large smooth table, large enough to cut a skirt on, a good sewing-machine, an ironing-board and an ironing-cushion. The latter you cannot buy but will have to make for yourself Cut a piece of heavy bed ticking 28 inches long and 18 inches wide. Make it into a bag by folding together and stitching along the two long sides. Cut old wool and cotton goods into small pieces until you have about four pounds. Soak them in water until thoroughly wet and then squeeze as much of the water out as possible. Fill the bag, making it very solid. Sew up the end and soak the whole pillow in water. While it is wet, pound it into shape (about like a loaf of bread) When dry cover with a piece of white cloth, and it is ready for use in pressing all seams of the waist and coat. By using this cushion you will not lose the curve of the seams.

Aside from the utensils mentioned you should have good pins and needles, a tracing-wheel and some tailors' chalk (you can buy this at a book store), a yardstick, a good pair of shears and a pair of button-hole scissors You should also have a good papier-mache bust form.

HOW TO MAKE A PAPIER-MACHE BUST FORM FOR ONE'S OWN DRESSMAKING

If you wish to do your own dressmaking you should fit up a bust form so that it will represent your own form exactly. To do this buy a good bust form your own bust measure. Draft a tight waist to your measure and have some one fit it to you very tightly, tighter than you could possibly wear it. Fit it down about the hips about 5 inches below the waist line and be sure it is perfect at every point. Use a very heavy lining material. Sew hooks and eyes quite close together down the back. Place this lining on your bust form, and by taking it off and on fill in all places where it does not fit the form, with layers of cotton put on very smoothly. Fill out until the lining is hard to hook on It should be as hard as possible, as you will wish to use it to fit your waists on. If it were left soft you might get your waist too tight. By placing a petticoat on this form you can hang your skirts on this form as well as fit your waists. Of course for the skirt the form will have to be on a standard. Any carpenter can easily make you one. Have him make a board just the size and shape of the bottom of the form. Place four legs on this board a little longer than your skirt measure. On the bottom of these legs fasten another board, large enough so that the standard will not tip over easily. Sew four tape loops to the sides of your bust form and put four brass-headed tacks in the edge of the top of the standard, leaving them out just enough to slip the tape over. This will keep the form from slipping off while you are working on it; at the same time you can remove it from the standard whenever you wish. You will find a bust form of this kind the most convenient thing you ever possessed.

LESSON III

You have learned the stitches and utensils used in sewing and dressmaking. We will now take up the actual work of making the gown.

Dressmaking is divided into four parts·

1. Planning the gown.
2. Drafting the gown.
3 Cutting the gown.
4. Finishing the gown.

We will take up the first:

PLANNING THE GOWN

The first thing to be thought of in planning the gown is the figure of the person for whom the gown is to be made   Is she tall and slender or short and stout? Is she light or dark? After settling these points, we must decide what sort of a gown would be best. For a small person the gown should have long straight lines to make her look tall. The tall slender person should have broken lines, lines running around, cutting up the length of the garment   For a short, stout person the back width should be broken so that it will look narrower.

We must also think of the coloring of the patron. All persons cannot wear the same colors. The complexion, color of the hair and eyes must be considered. For a fair complexion, lighter shades may be used. For the sallow complexion, brown, dark blue, olive green and black. We must also consider the time when the gown is to be worn. The garment for winter should be heavier than for summer. For those who cannot afford a

25

variety, dark colors should be worn. For those who can afford it, cream, tan or light grey is good   The garment for winter should be more severe in lines than the fluffy thin garment for summer wear.

We must also know for what occasion the dress is to be worn. Whether for a wedding, party, street wear or house

Having considered these points, we must now resort to the best fashion books to find our styles. It is never best to use extreme styles, as you will find that, if you do not, your gowns will stay in style much longer.

Sometimes you will have a patron who will choose from your books just the thing she should not wear. You must learn, if you wish to be a successful dressmaker, to influence her, in a tactful way, to choose some other style more suited to her form and coloring.

In planning the two-piece street gowns, no rule can be given, except that they are always planned on more severe lines than any other garment except the long coat. Both of these must be planned according to the prevailing style.

A party gown must be planned very differently from a street suit. For a very formal party gown, low neck and short sleeves should be used, except for young girls   Silks of delicate colors will be found the most suitable   These goods change nearly every year but a few standard ones may be found on the market, such as Chiffons, Nets, Crepe-de-Chine, Taffeta, Satin, etc. Velvet may always be used. For young girls, thin, soft wool or cotton goods are always good, such as Batiste, Crepe, Lawn, Taffeta and China silk may also be used

A party gown will permit of more trimming than any other kind of a gown. Plaiting, shirring and tucking may be used to good advantage on light materials   On the heavy materials like Velvet, Poplin or Brocade, heavy laces, appliques, jet trimmings or embroideries should be used

A gown for house wear, but for less formal wear than the party gown, used for afternoon receptions, dinners, etc , may be made of heavier materials: Henriettas, Velvets, Broadcloth, Voile, All Over Lace over Silk, Embroideries, etc They may be light in color or dark. They are made high-necked and with longer sleeves than the evening gown, usually reaching to the elbow, or half way between the elbow and wrist Or they may have long sleeves. Of course these garments must be planned according to the prevailing style, which will largely influence the trimming as well as the material. They should not be so heavily trimmed as the party gown. Sometimes a better style can be obtained by just a little touch here and there than by placing a large amount of trimming on the gown

Now we come to the Every Day Gown.

Almost any material may be used for this class of gown, except transparent materials. These are too dressy

In planning this gown we must consider the time of year when it is to be worn and in what climate Whether in the north or south.

For some years past the skirts with separate waists have been very popular, while they are still largely used, we are breaking away from this style and are going back again to the full dress of the same material

It is not best to suggest to your patron large figures Only a very slender figure can wear these When they are used they must be matched and usually cut all one way of the goods thus necessitating the buying of a large quantity of goods. Plain goods, small checks or tiny figures are best It will always improve your gown if you put in it a yoke of something light in color. This seems to relieve the complexion. The waist is usually lined, unless the goods is very heavy. A good quality of percaline or spun silk makes the best lining A drop skirt should be made to match the gown or of some color which blends well with it If the goods is thin enough to show the lining through, the lining of the waist and skirt should match in color. If not, a dark shade of grey always looks well and it will not crock. If your patron wishes a silk lining it should be of a good quality of Taffeta We do not recommend silk for waist linings

In deciding on the quantity of goods required for a gown, experience is the best teacher. You must think of three things. Width of goods, whether single or double fold, and the style of the gown.

The measures of the patron must be considered, but unless of unusual size this is not important. It usually takes from $5\frac{1}{2}$ to 9 yards of double width goods and from 14 to 20 yards of single width   The amount depends on how full the gowns are being made

Do not trust too much to what the clerk tells you. They are apt to give small measure

For the cotton lining $1\frac{1}{4}$ for the waist, $\frac{3}{4}$ for the sleeves and $5\frac{1}{2}$ yds. for the drop skirt will be all that is required. This varies with the style.

LESSON IV

THE chart consists of two pieces of cardboard, the edges of which are cut to form all the different curves needed to draft any garment The two pieces are hinged together so that by swinging one about on the other, the longer curves may be formed without using the long systems or charts used in many methods of drafting

Each curve is named according to its use and the ends of each curve are lettered. The intermediate points in the curves which are used, are also lettered One corner of the chart is left a true square so that it may be used to square one line with another. When point G is called for use any point inside the brace which will cause the curve to fall where it should. When in the directions for the drafts it says, square one line with another, it means that the one line must be exactly perpendicular with the other. One must form a right angle with the other.

To do the drafting one should be supplied with a good hard pencil, an eraser, and a good straight yardstick It will be found more convenient if the yardstick is sawed off at about 27 inches, as the yard length is rather unhandy to use.

The paper used may be of any size large enough to take the draft. A good quality manilla paper is the best.

The Chart

Open.

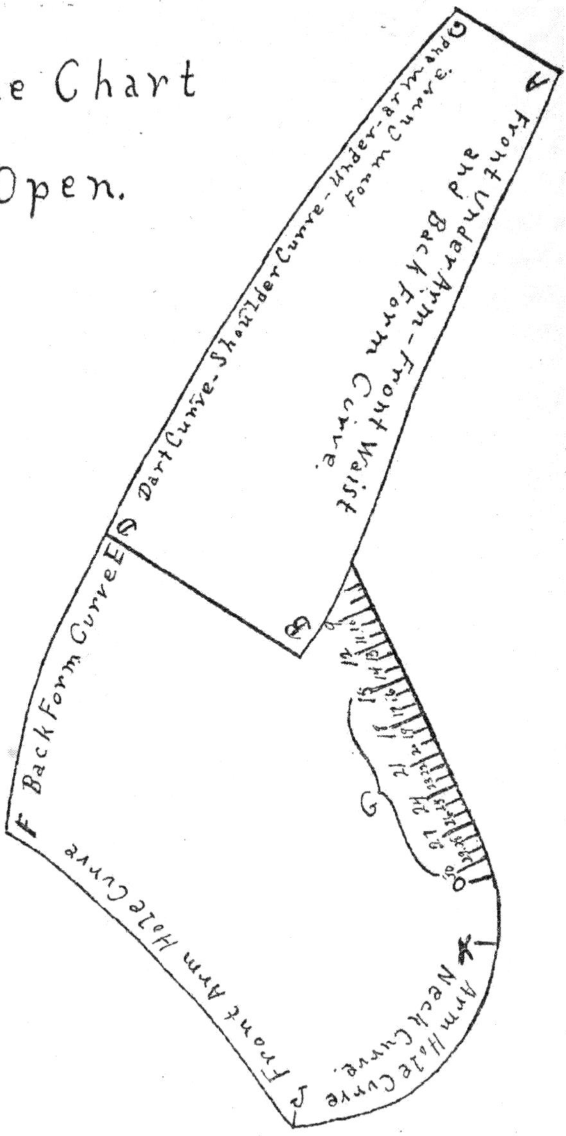

Front Under Arm and Back Form Curve.

Open-arm-Hole Form Curve.

Under arm Form Curve.

Dart Curve - Shoulder Curve -

Front Under-Arm - Front Waist

Back Form Curve

Front Arm Hole Curve

Arm Hole Curve

Neck Curve

The Chart Closed

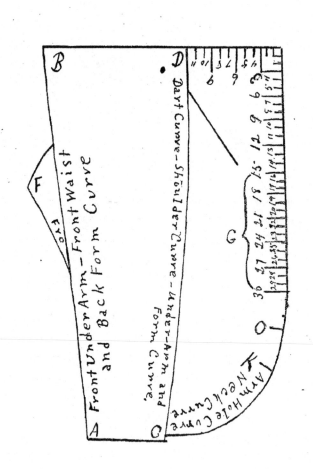

LESSON V

THE taking of measures is the most important part of drafting. If the measures are not taken correctly one can never hope to make a draft that will fit. The drafting of a garment is no different from the drafting of a house, a bridge, or a machine. If one line is inaccurate the entire draft will come wrong   You cannot be too careful in taking your measures. Above all things do not hurry and do not get excited when taking measures. If the person for whom the garment is being made does not wish to give time for you to take her measures you should not try to make the garment for her

Before you begin to take the measures, be sure that the patron is standing squarely on both feet.

The measures taken are. —

1. Waist measure.
2. Bust measure
3. Neck measure.
4. Armhole measure.
5. Under Arm measure.
6. Upper Front measure
7. Back Length measure.
8. Back Width measure
9. Front Length measure.
10. Arm Length measure.
11. Elbow measure.
12. Inside arm measure from armhole to bend of arm.
13 Hand measure.
14 Front Length of skirt.

32

15. Side Length of skirt.
16. Back Length of skirt.
17. Hip measure.

Waist Measure. — Stand in front of the patron. Place the tape-line about the smallest part of the waist. This measure should be very tight. Be sure you have the smallest part of the waist, and draw the measure as tight as a garment could be worn

After taking this measure, place a cord or tape at least ½ inch wide about the smallest part of the waist and do not remove it until you are through taking measures   It is a good plan to have a piece of tape about ¾ of an inch wide to the end of which has been fastened a small buckle   This can easily and quickly be adjusted about the waist and stay in place nicely

Bust Measure. — Stand back of the patron. Place the tape-line about the body under the arms and bring it together at the center back   Hold it firmly together with the right hand and step to the side of the patron. Allow the tape-line to slip through the fingers and bring it down in front over the highest part of the bust. Keep it well up under the arms and straight across the back   Allow the patron to draw a long breath and let the tape slip as she does this, so that it will be easy about the body

Neck Measure. — Have the patron remove her collar, never try to take the neck measure over a collar unless it is sewed to the dress, then take it tightly enough to allow for the collar. Place the tape-line about the neck where the collar should sew on, and measure about as tight as the collar would be worn. It is a good plan to ask the patron what size linen collar she wears This gives an idea as to whether you are getting your measure correct or not.

Armhole Measure. — Take this measure about the shoulder up high where the arm joins the body. Be sure to take it up over the high part of the bone. This measure should be taken tight, tighter than the armhole can be worn. The armhole can be cut out later, but if it comes too large in the draft and all the seams have to be taken in to make it right, the good lines which gave the waist style will be lost. Be sure to take it tight and be sure the patron's sleeve is not bunched up under the tape-line, under the arm

Before taking the next measure, place a piece of tape or cord about the patron so that it comes close up under the arms. Be very sure that it runs just straight around the body. It must not be allowed to dip down anywhere. Draw it rather tight. Do not pay any attention to the prominent part of the bust. Just have it perfectly straight about the body, close up under the arms.

Under Arm Measure. — Take this measure directly under the arm, from the top of this line, straight down to the bottom of the line at the bottom of the waist. Have the patron raise her arm just enough to take this measure. She must not raise it way up.

Upper Front Measure. — Place the end of the tape-line exactly on the prominent bone at the back of the neck. Bring the tape-line around the side of the neck close up to the neck and straight down in front to the top of the line which was placed around the body under the arms. Be sure that you bring the line down exactly straight from the side of the neck. It must not slant towards the back or front.

Back Length Measure. — Place the end of the tape-line on the prominent bone at the back of the neck and measure straight down the back to the bottom of the line about the smallest part of the waist. Be sure to take this measure straight down. It must not slant to right or left. Stand directly back of the patron to take this measure.

Back Width Measure. — This measure is taken across the back about the middle of the armholes. Be sure to get the measure wide enough. Do not pay any attention to the garment the patron has on. Measure out to where the arms join the body.

Both arms should be straight down at the sides, when this measure is taken.

Front Length Measure. — Place the end of the tape-line just where the neck should finish in front and measure straight down the front to the bottom of the line about the smallest part of the waist. Do not draw this measure tight. Make it just as you want the waist to set when finished.

Arm Length Measure. — Place the end of the tape-line at the front of the arm where the arm joins the body about on a straight line with the thumb Measure straight down the arm to the creases about the wrist joint. When taking this measure have the patron stretch the arm out at right angles to the body.

Elbow Measure. — Take this measure around the arm at the elbow with the arm bent at right angle. Be sure the tape-line is over the point of the elbow.

Inside Arm Measure from Armhole to Bend of Arm. — Take this measure from the same point you did the arm length measure down to the inside of the elbow. Have the patron bend her arm so that you can locate the exact stopping-place

Hand Measure. — This measure is taken about the hand with the fingers held straight out and the thumb close against the hand Take this measure just snug, not tight.

Front Length of Skirt. — Take this measure from the lower edge of the tape about the waist line at the exact middle of the front of the skirt, straight down the front of the skirt to the floor When you cut your pattern you can take off what you wish from this length It is best to take this measure to the floor, for it is difficult to tell just where to stop in taking it any other way

Side Length of Skirt. — Take this measure from the lower edge of the tape about the waist line, half way between the middle of the back and the middle of the front, straight down the side of the skirt to the floor.

Back Length of Skirt. — Take this measure from a point at the middle of the back, at the lower edge of the tape about

the waist line, straight down the middle of the back to the floor.

Take Hip Measure. — Take this measure about 5 or 6 inches below the waist line, straight around the prominent part of the hips. If the skirts are being worn very tight this measure should be taken snug. If the skirts are full take the measure just easy

If you are careful in taking these measures, your garments will need very little fitting, perhaps not any. Few of us, however, have perfect forms The method of drafting is worked out in inches, so it is bound to come right if the measures are taken correctly.

LESSON VI

MEASURES used for draft given: —

Waist measure . ..	25 inches
Neck measure	13½ inches
Armhole measure.	15 inches
Bust measure	39 inches
Back Width measure	13½ inches
Upper Front measure	10¾ inches
Front Length measure	15 inches
Under Arm measure	7¾ inches

1. Draw line A-B length of Back Length measure.

2. From A measure on line A-B Under Arm measure. Mark this point C.

3. At C square a line with line A-B.

4. From C measure on this line ½ of Bust measure. Mark this point D.

5. From C on line C-D measure ½ of Back Width measure. Mark this point E

6. At E square line with line C-D.

7 From E on this line measure 1-3 of Armhole measure. Mark this point F.

8. Measure ½ inch above point B. Mark this point G.

9. At G square a line with line G-A.

10. From G on this line measure 1½ inches. Mark this point H.

11. Place point O on the chart at point B and draw curve through H.

12. With curve D-C on the chart draw a curve through H and F.

39

13 Extend this curve beyond point F ½ inch. Mark this point I

14. From E measure on line C-D ¼ of Armhole measure. Mark this point J

15. Find a point half way between J and E. Mark this point K.

16. At point J square a line with line D-C.

17. From J on this line measure 2½ inches. Mark this point L.

18. Place point G on the chart at point I and draw curve · through K

19. Place point O on the chart at point L and draw curve through K.

20 Extend line E-F up 1¾ inches. Mark this point M.

21 At point M square a line with line E-M.

22. From M on this line measure 2 inches. Mark this point N.

23. Place point F on the chart at L and draw curve through N

24. Measure curve I-H.

25. From N measure the length of line I-H. Mark this point O.

26. Square a line with D-C so that it will pass through point O.

27. Measure from line D-C on this line, the Upper Front measure less what is used in the Back Neck   Mark this point P.

28. From point P measure down ¼ of neck measure. Mark this point Q

29 From Q measure up ½ inch.   Mark this point R.

30. At R square a line with line Q-R.

31 On this line from R measure 1-6 of Neck measure, and add ¼ inch. Mark this point S.

32. Place point J on the chart at S and draw curve through P.

SHIRT WAIST
DRAFT.

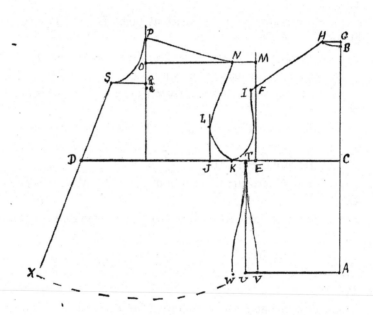

33. From point E on line C-D measure 1 inch to the left. Mark this point T.

34. At T square a line with line C-D and draw length of Under Arm measure   Mark this point U.

35   From U measure 1 inch to the right   Mark this point V.

36. Place point B on the chart at point T and draw curve through V.

37. Measure 1 inch to left of U.   Mark this point W.

38   Place point B on the chart at point T and draw curve through W.

39. Draw a line from S through D.

40. From S measure Front Length measure.   Mark this point X.

In cutting pattern allow all seams.

LESSON VII

DRAFTING THE SHIRT-WAIST SLEEVE

MEASURES used for draft given —

Arm Length measure	20 inches
Arm Length to Elbow	9½ inches
Elbow measure	12½ inches
Hand measure	˙8 inches
Armhole measure	15 inches

1. Draw line A-B Arm Length measure.

2. From A on line A-B measure Arm Length to Elbow. Mark this point C

3. At B square a line with line A-B.

4. At C square a line with line A-B.

5. At A square a line with line A-B.

6. From B measure on line drawn 1 inch. Mark this point D.

7 From C measure on line drawn ½ inch. Mark this point E.

8 Extend line drawn at A, 1 inch to the left   Mark this point F

9. Place point D on the chart at F and draw curve through E.

10. Connect points E and D with a straight line

11. From D measure 1 inch to the right. Mark this point G

12. From G measure to the right 2 inches more than the hand measure. Mark this point H.

13 From H measure to the right 1 inch   Mark this point I The distance between D and G and H and I is for gathers.

43

14. From E on line drawn measure ½ inch to the right. Mark this point J

15. From J measure the Elbow measure. Mark this point K.

16. From K to the right measure ½ inch. Mark this point L

17 Connect points L and I by straight line.

18 From A measure on line drawn the Armhole measure. Mark this point M.

19. From M measure to the right 2 inches. Mark this point N.

20. Extend line A-B above A 2½ inches. Mark this point O.

21. Square a line with line A-B at point O.

22. From A on line A-N measure 1½ inches. Mark this point P.

23. From M measure 3 inches to the left   Mark this point Q.

24 At P square a line with line A-N and mark the point R where this line touches the line from point O.

25 At Q square a line with line A-N and mark the point S where this line touches the line from O.

26. Place point D on the chart at L and draw curve through N

27 Place point G on the chart at point R and draw curve through point F.

28 Place point F on the chart at point S and draw a curve through point M. Continue the curve to point N.

29 Find the point half way between P and Q. Mark this point T.

30 Using T as a center and T-R as a radius draw an arc from R to S.

31. Find a point half way between G and H

32. From this point square a line with line B-I and draw ¾ of an inch long. Mark this point U.

33. Connect U with I and D using curve C-D on the chart.

Shirt Waist Sleeve.

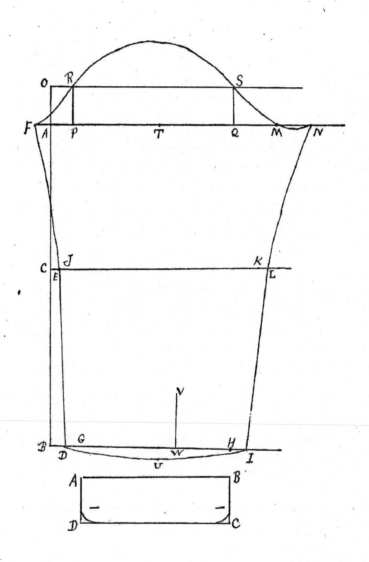

34. The cuff is drafted straight. Two inches longer than the hand measure and 3 inches wide   The lower corner may be curved if desired.

In cutting pattern allow all seams.

LESSON VIII

DRAFTING THE BLOUSE-WAIST

THE only changes made in the SHIRT-WAIST to make the BLOUSE-WAIST are —

1. Change the Under Arm seam from T to K.

2. Draw both the Under Arm seam for the back and the front, a straight slant from K through V and W.

3. The one through V is the Under Arm seam for the front and the one through W is the Under Arm of the back

4. Slant the middle back out 1½ inches

5 Add 4 inches to the bottom of the waist for blouse.

6. Hem the bottom with a narrow hem and run an elastic in it.

7. Cut away the front to a V shaped opening, line b, and finish neck with a large sailor collar.

LESSON IX

MANY people draft the sailor collar but it takes considerable time, so we will teach you a much quicker and simpler way and one which will not fail to fit the garment for which it is intended.

After the draft of the waist has been made and the pattern cut from paper, pin the shoulder seam together. Be sure to pin right on the line of each part. Spread the pattern out flat on the table and place the center back on a straight edge of the paper, and pin in place. Measure from the neck down the back the depth the collar is desired and square a line with the back line of the waist. Draw this line out as wide as the collar is to be across the back. Now decide how far you wish the collar to extend down the front and draw a line from the end of the line just drawn to the point in front. The best way to shape the outer edge of the collar is to cut the neck portion and then pin the pattern to the bust form and cut the edge any shape desired. You can see in this way just how the collar will look when finished. Any lay down collar may be cut in this way.

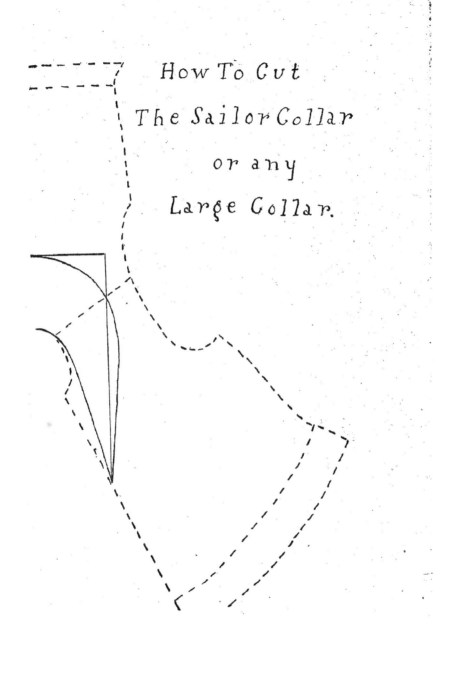

How To Cut
The Sailor Collar
or any
Large Collar.

LESSON X

To make the kimono waist   Trace off the draft of the shirt-waist on another piece of paper   Cut out, allowing seams every-where. Pin the back pattern to the front at the shoulder seam and spread out flat on the table. Take a large sheet of paper and place the pattern on it having the front line on a straight edge of the paper. This will bring the back bias. Draw a line from the neck out so that it will divide the Armhole into two very nearly equal parts. The back part will be a little smaller than the front. Draw two lines beginning about $1\frac{1}{2}$ inches below the Armhole on the under arm seam almost parallel to the line just drawn. They should come together very slightly towards the ends. Draw these lines as long as you wish the sleeve to be and connect them with a straight line. This forms the sleeve of the waist. It is never best to try to make the sleeves much more than elbow length, as it is difficult to raise the arm if they are much longer

In basting up the kimono waist, it should always be basted with seams on the right side until after it is tried on and fitted. After it has been thoroughly fitted, French seam with a very narrow seam so that it will turn well.

These waists may be as fancy as one wishes, having tucks or shirring over the shoulder. For a dress waist they are often made with a lining having a sewed in sleeve. This gives more freedom in raising the arm, and the sleeve is not so liable to tear out under the arm. For the Kimono Shirt-Waist the sleeve should be quite loose.

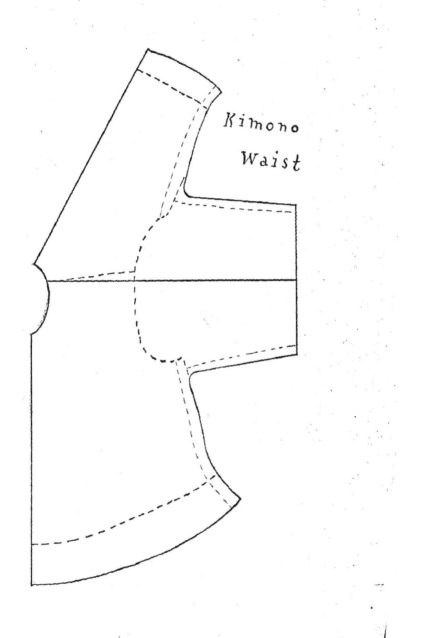

Kimono
Waist

LESSON XI

You have learned to draft the Shirt-Waist and the Shirt-Waist Sleeve. We will now take up the making and finishing of the shirt-waist.

After the draft has been made, trace off each part of the waist on another piece of paper. Cut out, allowing seams everywhere. This gives you an exact pattern to use in cutting out the waist.

Before using cotton goods it should be shrunk. Place in warm water over night and when nearly dry press. If the goods is colored put some salt in the water.

Put all plaits and tucks in the goods before laying on the pattern. If there is no up or down to the goods, a piece long enough to cut both fronts may be cut off and the two tucked at once.

All trimming should be put on after the waist is cut out but before it is basted up.

If the waist is to be tailor made, it will have a box plait down the front. To make this, cut a straight strip from the edge of the goods wide enough to allow for turning under. This piece should be just the length of one side of the front. Baste the piece on the edge of the cloth from which the right side front is to be cut, and stitch ¼ inch from both edges. (See Ill.) Your tucks must be planned to come at the right distance from this plait. If you only want to tuck yoke deep, fold the goods you have cut off for fronts together in the center crosswise. (See Ill.) Measure on each part, from the fold down, just how deep you wish the yoke to come and tuck between the marks.

If you wish the tucks to grow shorter towards the armholes,

53

mark the goods slanting. To put in the tucks, fold the cloth lengthwise just where you want the tucks to come. Measure the width you want the tucks and put in with a running stitch or on the machine   Press the tucks before you try to cut the waist. When you fold the goods together to cut the fronts, be sure that the tucks for each piece lie exactly on top of each other. Cut from the goods, marking all seams with the tracing wheel. Baste up and try on. Baste on the collar band, after stitching the seams of the waist   To cut the collar band. use your tape-line to draw a circle   Take a radius of 10 inches. Use the corner of the paper for the center of the circle and draw parts of two circles 1 inch apart. Measure off enough length, from the edge of the paper on the lower circle, for ½ the neck measure. Cut out the pattern and allow seams on both sides when you cut it from the cloth.

To finish the bottom of the shirt-waist sleeve, if tailor made. Make a cuff of three thicknesses of goods, if cotton, or with an interlining of cotton, if wool, 3½ inches wide and 10½ inches long, straight of the goods lengthwise   Slash the sleeves up on line W-V about 4 inches   Baste on the under edge of this opening a strip of goods about 1½ inches wide, having turned in the edges (see Ill. 1) so that it projects from the opening

Lay the sleeve on the table right side up, and place over this piece just sewed on a piece about 2½ inches wide which has been folded in the middle lengthwise and both edges turned in   Place the lengthwise fold of this piece so that it just covers the under seam. The upper turned in edge of the piece will come on the right side of the sleeve and the under edge on the wrong side of the sleeve just opposite the other   Baste into place and stitch. It looks best to finish the upper end of this piece, which comes on the right side of the sleeve, to a point   Stitch about the point on the machine   (See Ills 1 and 2.) Stitch up the sleeve   Gather the bottom, leaving 1½ inches each side of the seam plain. Baste the pieces of the cuff together wrong side out, leaving one long side open. Turn and baste the edge on the right side, having the edge very smooth and even   Notch the open side of the cuff about 1 inch from the center. Baste to the bottom of the sleeve, having the shortest part come on the under side of the sleeve

In basting to the sleeve have the right side of the cuff against the right side of the sleeve. Only baste two of the three pieces of which the cuff is made, at the first basting, leaving the third, or lining, loose   Turn the cuff down and turn in the edge of the lining and baste in place. Stitch all four sides of the cuff on the right side very near the edge. Gather the top of the sleeve from about 2 inches from the seam on the upper side, and 5½ inches from the seam on the under side. Sew in and bind the armhole, after having tried on the waist for the last time. Work a buttonhole in each end of the neck band, one in the center of the back and one at each end of the cuffs   They may also be worked down the front if desired. Finish the bottom of the waist as the patron wishes. Some like the fullness stitched in, while others want it left loose so that they can place it where they wish when the waist is worn.

The fancy shirt-waist should fasten in the back instead of the front. The same draft is used. It may be tucked yoke deep across the front and down the back, tucked in clusters with insertion of lace or embroidery between or any sort of ornaments placed on the front

In making collars and yokes of lace insertion, cut a correct pattern from white paper. Baste the rows of lace on this and stitch together on the machine. Tear the paper away and you have your yoke and collar just the desired shape.

All tucks must be placed in the goods before it is cut.

For the fancy waist the sleeves may be made as fancy as one wishes. They may be short or long as the style demands   For the short sleeve, the draft given may be used by laying a plait lengthwise in the pattern thus taking out the gathers, leaving only a few at the armhole. A Leg O'Mutton sleeve may be made from this same draft by laying a plait lengthwise beginning at

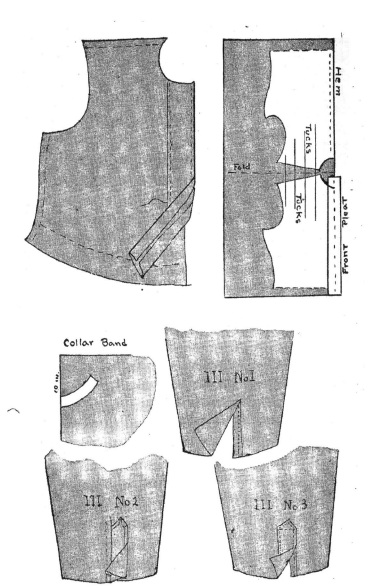

Hem

Tucks

Fold

Tucks

Front Pleat

Collar Band

III No1

III No2

III No3

the bottom and letting it out gradually towards the top. The shirt-waist draft is used to make the shirt-waist dress Combined with the seven gored skirt it makes a fine shirt-waist suit.

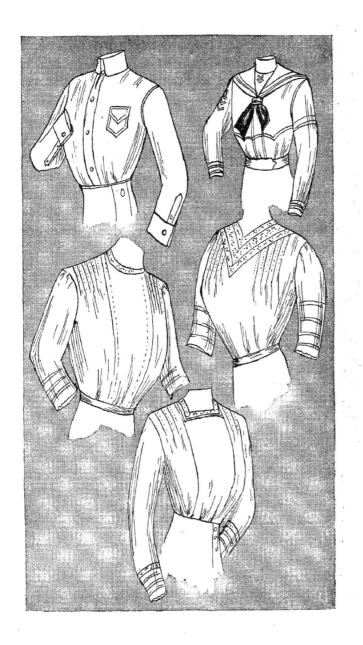

LESSON XII

MEASURES used for draft given —

Waist measure	25	inches
Neck measure	13½	inches
Armhole measure	15	inches
Bust measure .	39	inches
Back Width measure	13½	inches
Under Arm measure	7¾	Inches
Front Length measure	15½	inches
Upper Front measure	10¾	inches
Back Length measure	16	inches

1. Draw line A-B length of back.

2. From A measure the Under Arm measure. Mark this point C.

3. Measure up from B ½ inch. Mark this point D.

4. Square line D-E with line D-C at point D.

5. D to E is 1½ inches.

6. Place point O on the chart at point B and draw curve through point E.

7. At C square a line with line A-B.

8. From C on this line measure ½ of Bust measure Mark this point F.

9. From C on line C-F measure ½ of Back width. Mark this point G.

10. At G square a line with line C-F.

11. From point G measure on this line 1-3 of Armhole measure. Mark this point H.

12. Place I half way between G and H.

59

13 With curve D-C on the chart, draw curve through E and H.

14. Extend line G-H above point H $1\frac{3}{4}$ inches.   Mark this point J.

15. At J square a line with line G-J.

16. From J on this line measure 2 inches.   Mark this point K.

17. Measure from G on line C-F $\frac{1}{4}$ of Armhole measure. Mark this point L.

18 Square a line at L with line C-F and draw $2\frac{1}{2}$ inches long.   Mark this point M.

19 Find a point half way between L and G.   Mark this point N.

20 Extend curve E-H $\frac{1}{2}$ inch beyond H.

21. Place point G on the chart at the end of this curve, holding the chart to the left, and draw a curve through point N.

22. Place point O on the chart at point M and draw a curve through M and N.

23 Place point F on the chart at point M, holding chart to the left, and draw curve through points M and K.

24. Measure the full length of curve E-H and mark the same distance from K on line K-O   Mark this point O.

25. Square a line with line C-F so that it will run through point O

26 Measure up on this line from line C-F the length of Upper Front measure less what is used in the back of the neck. Mark this point P.

27 With curve D-C on the chart draw a curve through P and K

28. From P measure down $\frac{1}{4}$ of Neck measure   Mark this point Q

29 Square a line at Q with line P-Q.

30 Measure from Q, 1-6 of the Neck measure and add $\frac{1}{4}$ inch   Mark this point R

31. Place point J on the chart at R and draw a curve through P.

32. Measure on line R-F the Front Length measure. Mark this point S.

33. Square a line with line C-F at point N.

34. Measure down on this line the Under Arm measure. Mark this point T.

35. Draw a line from T to A.

36. Measure from A on line A-T ¾ of an inch. Mark this point U.

37. Draw line B-U.

38. Find a point half way between T and U. Mark this point W.

39. From point W measure to the right 2¼ inches. Mark this point V.

40. Place point F on the chart at a point ¾ of an inch below I and draw with curve F-C on the chart, a curve through V.

41. Place point D on the chart at the point where curve I-V crosses line C-F and draw curve through point W.

42. Measure towards the right from T on line A-T 1 inch Mark this point X.

43. With curve D-C on the chart draw a curve through points N and X.

44. From point T measure towards the left 1¼ inches Mark this point Y.

45 Place point B on the chart at point N and draw curve through points N and Y, holding the chart to the left

46. Place point C on the chart at S and draw curve through Y.

47 From point S measure towards the right 1 inch. Mark this point Z.

48. Place point B on the chart at point F and draw curve through Z.

49 From Z towards the right measure 1¾ inches. Mark this point a.

50. To find out how much to take out in the darts, — Find on the tape-line ½ of Waist measure. Place this point at U. Now

measure from U to V, W to X and Z to a. Place the point
which falls at a, at point Y and with what is left measure towards point Z. Mark this point The distance from this point
to a is what must be taken out in darts, less the space we leave
between the darts (b to d), which should be about 1 inch. The
front dart is always made larger than the back one.

51. From a to b is width of front dart. In this case 3 inches.

52. From d to e is width of back dart In this case 2 inches

53 c is half way between a and b and f is half way between
d and e.

54. From c through a point on the shoulder line 1 inch from
P, draw a line.

55. Measure up on this line, from point c, 8 inches for a
tall person and 6 inches for a short person. Mark this point g.
(8 ins. is used in this draft)

56. From point g measure towards the right 3 inches exactly
parallel with line C-F. Mark this point h.

57. With curve C-D on the chart, draw curves a-g, b-g, h-d,
e-h.

58. Measure down from points U, T, f, c, and Z, 5 inches.

59. Connect points U and i.

60. From a point half way between V and W, square a line
with line A-T and draw 5 inches long. Mark this point j

61. Connect point j with V and j with W, with straight lines.

62. Extend line N-T down 5 inches. Mark this point k.

63. Connect point k with X

64. Measure to the right of k, 1 inch, mark this point l.

65. Place point F on the chart at Y and draw curve
through l.

66. Make the distance from m to n and o to p about ½ less
than from e to d and a to b.

67. Connect a and e with a straight line.

68. Draw line Z-q straight down 5 inches

69. Connect m and e, n and d, o and b, p and a.

NOTE — In drafting any of the waists below the waist line,

Tight Waist Draft

With Back Form.

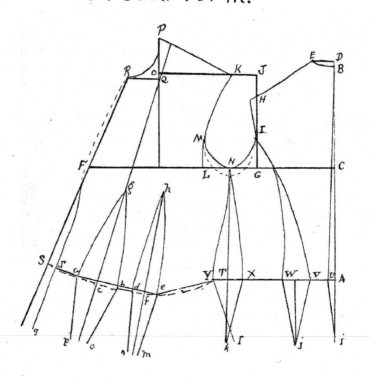

it will be found necessary to change the measures for different persons. Some who have very small wàist measure will have large hips, while some with large waist measure will have small hips   Use the hip measure and change each measure a little so that the draft 5 inches below the waist line will be the exact hip measure

In cutting out the Armhole of any waist, remember that you took the measure tighter than it could be worn, so it must be cut out more than the draft.   See dotted line on draft.

In cutting the pattern from the draft allow seams everywhere.

LESSON XIII

DRAFTING THE WAIST WITHOUT BACK FORMS

MEASURES used in draft given —

Waist measure	25 inches
Neck measure ..	13½ inches
Armhole measure .	15 inches
Bust measure	39 inches
Back Width measure	13½ inches
Under Arm measure	7¾ inches
Front Length measure .	15½ inches
Upper Front measure	10¾ inches
Back Length measure. ..	16 inches

1. Draw line A-B length of back.

2. From B to D is ½ inch.

3. At D square a line with line A-B

4 On this line measure from point D 1½ inches. Mark this point E.

5. Place point O on the chart at point B and draw curve through E

6. At point C square a line with A-B.

7. On this line measure from point C ½ the Bust measure. Mark this point F.

8. From point C on line C-F measure ½ of back width   Mark this point G.

9. At point G square a line with line C-F

10. On this line measure from G, 1-3 of Armhole measure. Mark this point H.

11. Place point D on the chart at E and draw curve through H and extend curve ½ inch beyond H

12. Measure on line G-H, from point H, 1 3-4 inches. Mark this point I.

13 From G on line C-F measure ¼ Armhole measure. Mark this point J.

14 Find a point half way between J and G. Mark this point L.

15. At point J square a line with line C-F.

16 Measure on this line from J, 2½ inches. Mark this point M.

17. Place point G on the chart at the end of curve E-H and draw a curve through point L

18 Place point O on the chart at M and draw a curve through L.

19. Place point F on the chart at M and draw a curve through K.

20. Extend line I-K to the left of K

21. On this line measure from K the same length as the curve from E extended through H   Mark this point N.

22. Square a line with line C-F so that it will pass through N.

23. Measure on this line from line C-F the Upper Front measure, less the Back Neck measure. Mark this point O

24 With curve D-C draw a curve through K and O.

25. From O measure down ¼ the Neck measure. Mark this point P.

26 At P square a line with line O-P.

27 On this line measure from P, 1-6 of the Neck measure and add ¼ inch. Mark this point Q

28 Place point J on the chart at Q and draw curve through point O

29. Draw a straight line from Q through F.

30 On this line measure from Q, the Front Length measure Mark this point R

31. Find a point half way between J and L. Mark this point S

32. At point S, square a line with line C-F.

33. Measure on this line from line C-F the Under Arm measure. Mark this point T.

34. Connect T and A with a straight line

35. From A measure on this line 1 inch. Mark this point U.

36. Connect U and B.

37. Find a point half way between U and T and measure ½ inch to the right of this point. Mark this point V.

38. Place point C on the chart at V and with curve C-F on the chart, draw a curve through point G.

39. From V measure 1 inch to the left. Mark this point W.

40. Place point B on the chart at G and draw a curve through W.

41. Measure 1 inch to the right of T. Mark this point X.

42. With curve D-C on the chart draw a curve from X to S.

43. Measure 1½ inches to the left of T.

44. Place point C on the chart at X, and draw curve to S.

45. Measure from U to V and from W to X. This shows how much of the Waist measure has been used in the back.

46. From R measure to the right ½ inch. Mark this point Z.

47. Place point A on the chart at Z and draw curve touching line F-R.

48. From point Y measure towards point Z what is left of the Waist measure after taking out what is used in the back. Mark this point

49. Measure the distance from this point to Z. This gives what must be taken out in darts to bring the garment in to the proper Waist measure, in this case 4¾ inches.

50. We will make the Front Dart 2¾ inches and the back one 2 inches

51. Place point C on the chart at R and draw curve C-F through Y.

52. From Z measure 2 inches   Mark this point a

53. From a measure 2¾ inches (Front Dart). Mark this point b.

54. From b, measure 1 inch. Mark this point c.

55. From c measure 2 inches (Back Dart). Mark this point d.

56 Find a point half way between a and b. Mark this point e.

57. From a point 1 inch to the right of O draw a straight line through e

.   58 From e measure up on this line 8 inches for a tall person and 6 for a short person (we use 8 inches in this draft).   Mark this point f.

59. With curve D-C on the chart draw a curve from f to a and from f to b.

60 Find a point half way between c and d. Mark this point g

61. Measure from f, 3 inches to the right and parallel to line C-F. Mark this point h

62. Draw a straight line connecting h and g

63. With curve D-C on the chart connect h and d and h and c.

64. To form the bottom of the waist. —

Measure down 5 inches from A. Mark this point i. Connect U and i with a straight line.

65. Find a point half way between V and W   At this point square a line with line A-T.

66. Measure down on this line 5 inches. Mark this point j   Connect j and V, and j and W with straight lines.

67. Extend line S-T down 5 inches   Mark this point k. Connect k and X with a straight line.

68. Measure 1 inch to the right of k. Mark this point l.

69. Place point F on the chart at Y, and draw curve to l.

70. Extend line h-g down 5 inches   Mark this point m.

71 Using ½ the distance from c to d as a measure and placing the middle of this distance at m, mark points either side of m — o and n.

72. Connect n with d and o with c by straight lines. Extend line e-f down 5 inches. Mark this point p.

Tight Waist Draft

Without Back Form.

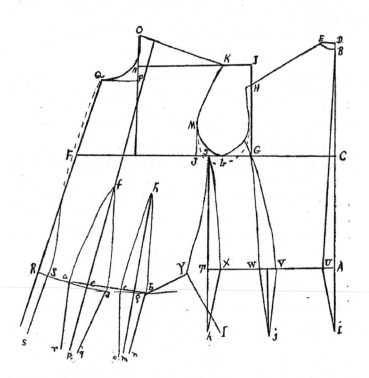

73 With p as a center, using ½ the distance from a to b, mark points r and q.

74. Connect r and a, and q and b with straight lines.

75. Extend curve Z straight down 5 inches.

76. Connect a and d with a straight line.

NOTE — For a person with a very large waist measure it is best to make the distance from b to c a little more, say 1½ inches, or even 2 inches.

This waist is the best one to use for linings as the back form seam is apt to show especially where the goods is thin.

LESSON XIV

DRAFTING THE WAIST WITH FRENCH FORMS

MEASURES used in this draft —

Waist measure	25 inches
Neck measure	13½ inches
Armhole measure	15 inches
Bust measure	39 inches
Back Width measure	13½ inches
Under Arm measure	7¾ inches
Front Length measure	15½ inches
Upper Front measure	10¾ inches
Back Length measure	16 inches

1. Draw line A-B the length of Back measure

2. Measure from A the Under Arm measure. Mark this point C.

3. B to D is ½ inch.

4. At D square a line with A-D.

5. Measure from D on this line 1½ inches Mark this point E.

6. Place point O on the chart at B and draw curve through E

7. At C square a line with line A-B

8 C to F is ½ of Bust measure

9. From C on line C-F measure ½ of Back Width measure. Mark this point G.

10 At G square a line with line C-F.

11. Measure on this line from point G, 1-3 of Armhole measure Mark this point H.

12. Place point D on the chart at E and draw curve through H Extend curve ½ inch beyond H.

13. Extend line G-H above H $1\frac{3}{4}$ inches. Mark this point I.

14. At I square a line with line G-I.

15. On this line measure from I, 2 inches. Mark this point J.

16. From G on line C-F measure $\frac{1}{4}$ of the Armhole measure. Mark this point K.

17. Find a point half way between K and G

18. At K square a line with line C-F.

19. Measure on this line, $2\frac{1}{2}$ inches from K. Mark this point M.

20. Measure full length of curve E-H and mark the same measure from J on line I-J, extended   Mark this point N.

21. Place point G on the chart at point H and draw curve through L.

22. Place point O on the chart at M and draw a curve through L.

23. Place point F on the chart at M and draw curve through J. Place point D on the chart at O and draw curve through J.

24. Square a line with line C-F so that it will pass through point N.

25. Measure on this line from line C-F the Upper Front measure, less what is used in the Back Neck   Mark this point O.

26. From O measure on this line $\frac{1}{4}$ the Neck measure   Mark this point P

27. At P square a line with line O-P

28. Measure on this line from P 1-6 of Neck measure.   Add $\frac{1}{4}$ inch. Mark this point Q.

29. Place point J on the chart at Q and draw curve through O.

30. From Q draw line through F.

31. From Q on this line measure the Front Length measure. Mark this point R.

32. At L square a line with line C-F.

33. Measure on this line from L the Under Arm measure. Mark this point S.

34. Connect S and A with a straight line.

35. From A on this line measure ¾ of an inch. Mark this point T.

36. Connect T and B with a straight line.

37. Measure on the shoulder curve 2 inches from the Armhole. Mark this point U.

38 Find a point half way between T and S and measure ½ inch to the left of this point. Mark this point V.

39 From V measure 1¼ inches to the right. Mark this point W.

40. Connect U and W with a straight line.

41. Place point C on the chart at V and let point D touch line U-W. Draw curve.

42. Measure to the right of S, 1 inch. Mark this point X

43. Place point D on the chart at L and draw curve through X

44. Measure to the left of S 1½ inches. Mark this point Y

45. Place point A on the chart at Y and draw curve through L.

46. Measure from T to W and from V to X. This shows how much of the waist measure has been used in the back.

47. Measure from Y towards R what is left of the waist measure, after taking out what was used in the back. Mark this point.

48. Measure the distance from this point to point R. This gives the amount to be taken out in the dart to bring the waist into the correct waist measure. In this case it is 4½ inches.

49. Place point C on the chart at R and draw curve through Y, using curve C-F on the chart

50. Measure from J on curve J-O 2 inches. Mark this point Z.

51. Measure from R 2½ inches Mark this point a.

52. Connect a and Z with a straight line.

Tight Waist with French Forms.

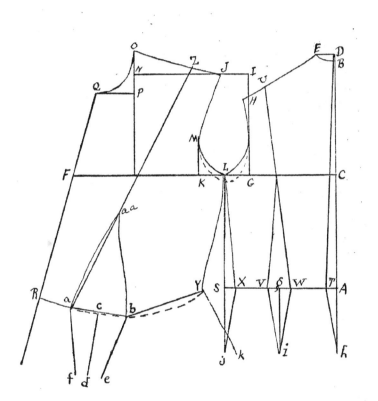

53. Measure from a on line a-Z 8 inches for a tall person and 6 inches for a short person. Mark this point aa.

54. With curve D-C on the chart connect a with aa

55. Measure to right of a 4½ inches (dart). Mark this point b.

56. Place point B on the chart at aa and draw curve through b.

57. Find a point half way between a and b. Mark this point c.

58. Connect a and b with a straight line.

59. At c square a line with line a-b, and measure from c, 5 inches. Mark this point d.

60. Find ½ the distance from a to b and with d as a center, mark points e and f.

61 Connect e and b with a straight line.

62. Connect a and f with a straight line.

63. Extend line Q-R below R 5 inches.

64. Connect b and Y with a straight line.

65 Extend line A-B below A 5 inches. Mark this point h.

66. Connect h and T with a straight line

67. Find a point half way between V and W. Mark this point g.

68 Square a line at g, with line A-S and measure down from g, 5 inches. Mark this point i.

69 Connect W and i with a straight line, also connect V and i.

70. Extend line L-S below S 5 inches Mark this point j

71. Measure to the right of j 1 inch. Mark this point k.

72. Place point F at Y and draw curve through k.

73 Connect X and j with a straight line.

In cutting pattern allow all seams.

LESSON XV

WE have finished planning the gown, and have learned to draft the different kinds of waists We will now take up the Cutting, Fitting and Making of the waist.

After making the draft you should trace, with the tracing wheel each piece of the draft off on another piece of paper, and cut out each part allowing seams everywhere. ½ inch seam should be allowed at the Armhole, Neck and Back Form pieces. 1 inch at the shoulder and 1½ inches at the Under Arm seams, down the back and at the front. This much need not be allowed at the back unless the waist is to be open there. BE VERY CAREFUL TO MARK THE TRUE WAIST LINE ON EACH PIECE.

After the correct pattern has been cut from the paper, spread the lining out on a table. Lay the different parts of the pattern on the lining to the best advantage to save cloth. BE VERY CAREFUL THAT THE TRUE WAIST LINE OF EACH PIECE IS ON THE STRAIGHT OF THE CLOTH CROSSWISE, so that they will not stretch off on the bias when finished BE SURE TO TRACE THE TRUE WAIST LINE OF EACH PIECE BEFORE YOU PICK UP THE PATTERN, also trace all seams.

We now have our waist lining all cut out and are ready to baste it up. Begin by basting up the back seam, if the waist is to open in front, if not this seam will not be basted. Next baste the side forms next to the back, taking care not to stretch the seam where it is circling. Last of all the second form seams. In basting all seams the pieces must always be pinned together at the waist line before you begin to baste and they should always be made to come out even at the armhole It is always best to pin the seam the full length before you begin to baste.

Baste the darts in the front pieces, pinning the waist line first. After these are basted, baste the under arm seams and shoulder seams. Be very careful not to lose the little curves in the shoulder seams In basting the lining, do not crush or soil it. It will never fit well if you do Now the waist is all basted and we are ready to have our patron come for a first fitting If you have learned to take your measures correctly there should be very few, if any changes to make I have put many linings on persons where there were no changes to make at all. Of course if a person is out of shape in any way, their lining must be fitted.

Your patron has come to be fitted. Place the lining on her and pin up very carefully, following the tracing either in front or in the back as the case may be.

To fit the waist. — If the neck is a little tight, cut out a small seam If very tight, open the shoulder seam a little way and let out If the lining is too tight or too loose at the bust, it should be taken in or let out at the under arm seam. If the waist draws from the neck to the armhole, open the shoulder seam at the neck and let out in front Be sure the waist is loose enough between the shoulders and that it is not too loose at the armhole If it is, take in the form seams a little.

After the lining has been thoroughly fitted, all the seams should be stitched and pressed open on the pressing cushion, after they have all been trimmed to about $\frac{1}{2}$ inch. Clip each seam $\frac{1}{2}$ inch below and above the waist line. Be very careful not to stretch the seams or lose any of the curves in pressing. It is the curve which gives style to the waist.

We are ready now to bone the lining. Use the best quality of Featherbone. Sometimes real whalebone is used, but it has grown very expensive and most dressmakers now substitute Featherbone It will take about 3 or 4 yards of the bone Use silk thread for stitching it in, and the longest stitch your machine will make. You can get the Featherbone in either silk or cotton. The quality of the gown will determine which to use The style of the gown will determine just how far below the waist line the bones should be allowed to run   If the waist is to be worn outside the skirt, it should be boned ½ inch at back and sides and 1 inch in front below the waist line   If a princess gown or a one-piece gown of any sort, the bones should run 3 or 4 inches below the waist line   In this case the waist should be fitted very snug about the hips, so that the ends of the bones will not stick out. The bones for each seam will be of a different length   The back center bone should be 6 or 7 inches long above the waist line. Each bone should grow shorter towards the under arm seam.   This bone should be the shortest of all, about 4 or 5 inches above the waist line   The bones for the darts should be about an inch shorter than the dart so that it will not show   The front bone should be the same as the dart bone   If the waist opens in the front there will be a bone of equal length on each side of the front. These bones should be run in the hem and stitched, and not placed on the outside as on the seams. If the waist opens in the back, the two bones should be run in the hems in the back instead of in the front, then the front bone will be stitched on the same as the others.

Cut the bones about 1½ inches longer than you want them   Rip the covering back from each end about ½ inch and cut the bone off. Turn the covering down over the end and fasten securely but neatly. Pin the upper end to the seam where you want it to come, and spring the bone so that the lower end will come where it should   The bones are placed on the inside of the waist, and not between the lining and the outside   Place under the machine, holding the bone in place so that it will follow the seam. The lining will stretch to the bone   Always begin stitching at the top of the bone and 1 inch from the end   This leaves 1 inch of the bone loose at the upper end, and prevents the end showing when the waist is worn   After the bones are all stitched in, draw the ends of the threads through on the right side of the waist and tie securely. Sew hooks and eyes on the lining and it is finished. No 2 hooks and eyes with a hump are best, black for dark colors and white for light colors.

The hooks are sewed on the right-hand side of the front when the waist opens in front. If in the back they are placed on the left-hand side. Pin the two sides of the lining together, being sure that the true waist lines are even. Mark with pins the place where each hook and each eye should go, making them about 1¼ inches apart. Both the hooks and eyes must be sewed on the wrong side of the lining, the eyes coming out just far enough to let the hooks slide in. If the gown is to have a fancy yoke, do not sew hooks and eyes where this will come, as the lining will be cut away here, after we get the outside ready to place on it.

We are ready now to cut the outside. If this is to follow rather closely the shape of the lining, we can use the same pattern for cutting. However, if it is to be very different, we must cut a new pattern, always leaving the shoulder and armhole the same as the lining. Pin the pattern to your bust form and shape the front or back so that it looks just as you wish it to look in the finished waist. In making this pattern for the outside, all fullness of every kind must be put in the paper pattern.

When the pattern for the outside has been prepared, spread the goods out on the table and lay all the pieces of the pattern on, being careful to have the true waist line on the straight of the goods crosswise. Sometimes, however, small checks and plaids are cut on the bias. In this case the true waist line should be on a true bias of the goods. In cutting the outside back the form pieces are not used The back is cut all in one piece, if the waist opens in front, if not, then it is cut in two pieces. It is best to pin all the pieces of the back pattern, which are used to cut the lining, together just as you sewed them for the lining, and use this for a pattern for cutting the outside back. Cut the goods from the wrong side, and before lifting the pattern mark all seams with tailor's chalk. If two pieces are cut at once, follow the lines made on one side with pins. Turn over and follow the pins with the chalk. Run a thread in each piece marking the true waist line before taking up the pattern. When the outside is all cut, pin the under arm seams together, beginning with the true waist line, and baste Do the same with the shoulder seams These are all the seams we have in the outside. These seams should be just like the lining, as, if we made any changes in fitting the lining we should have made the same in the outside pattern. We can therefore stitch these seams. Trim the seams to about ½ inch and overcast each side. Press open on the pressing cushion The under arm seams should be clipped above and below the waist line.

Now place the lining on the bust form and fill out with soft paper wherever it is larger than the form. Place the outside on it Pin the shoulder seams in the outside to the shoulder seams of the lining, and the under arm seams at the armhole to the under arm seam of the lining. Pin securely all about the armhole, being sure that the outside is smooth. If the outside is cut kimono, it will not fasten anywhere to the lining, except at the bottom of the waist. Of course all waists fasten to the lining where the collar sews on or at the bottom of a fancy yoke. When the outside is kimono it should be left to blouse a little under the arms to give freedom in raising the arms.

Arrange fullness in the outside just as you wish it to be when finished. Pin it, leaving the basting until you have had another fitting. Put all trimming in place while it is on the form

A very good way when a fancy waist is being made is to cut the pattern out of old cloth Pin it to the lining on the bust form and keep changing it a little here and there until it looks just as you wish it to when finished. Use this cloth as a pattern to cut from the goods. With a little practice you will get so you can cut any waist you see. If the dress is being made of thin wash goods, of course it will not have a lining, unless your patron wishes one Some people wish their summer gowns made on a lining. For this purpose we use a thin lining lawn. When no lining is used it is nearly always best to use the shirt-waist pattern instead of the tight lining pattern. In this case arrange all tucks and fullness of every kind in your pattern. Cut from

the goods. Stitch up the seams and place on the bust form to arrange fullness as it should be when finished. These waists must be made with a kind of fullness that can be stitched in, such as shirring, tucking, etc.

Our waist is ready for a second fitting, but we will lay it away while we prepare the rest of the gown, before we ask our patron to come again.

LESSON XVI

DRAFTING THE COAT OR LINING SLEEVE

MEASURES used for draft given —

Arm Length measure	20 inches
Arm Length to bend of Elbow .	9½ inches
Armhole measure	15 inches
Elbow measure	12½ inches
Hand measure .	8 inches

1. Draw line A-B length of Arm measure.

2. From point A measure on line A-B length of Arm to bend of Elbow   Mark this point C.

3 At C square a line with line A-B

4. From C measure on this line 2 inches. Mark this point D.

5. Place point D on the chart at D and draw curve through A.

6 Place point D on the chart at D and draw curve through B.

7. From D measure ½ Elbow measure   Mark this point E.

8. Measure 1¼ inches to right of E. Mark this point G.

9. Measure 1¼ inches to left of E. Mark this point F.

10 Measure ¼ inch to right of points F and G. Mark these points H and I

11. At point B square a line with line A-B.

12. Measure from B on this line ½ of Hand measure   Mark this point J.

13. Measure ¼ inch to the right of J. Mark this point K.

14. At K square a line with line B-K and measure 1 inch from K. Mark this point L.

15. Connect points L and B with a straight line.

85

16. Measure to the left of L 1¼ inches ·Mark this point M.

17. Connect points H and M with a straight line.

18. Connect points I and L with a straight line.

19. Place point F on the chart at G and hold chart so that point J falls on line I-L, draw curve.

20 Place point F on the chart at F and hold so that point J falls on line H-M, draw curve. This forms the Elbow.

21. Measure the line G-L and extend the line F-M below M so that it is the same length as line G-L. Mark this point N.

22. Connect N and B with a straight line.

23. At point A square a line with line A-B.

24. From A measure on this line ½ the Armhole measure. Mark this point O

25. Measure 2 inches to the right of O. Mark this point P.

26 Measure 2 inches to the left of O. Mark this point Q.

27. Extend line A-B above A˙ 2½ inches. Mark this point R

28 At R square a line with line R-B.

29 On this line measure from R 1½ inches. Mark this point S.

30. At point Q square a line with line A-P. Mark this point T.

31 At point P square a line with line A-P. Mark this point U.

32. Place point G on the chart at T and hold so that the curve just touches line A-P. Draw curve and continue it to point A.

33 Place point G on the chart at S and draw curve through A.

34. Using Q as a center and Q-S as a radius, draw curve through points S and U.

35. Connect points T and F with a straight line.

36. Connect U and G with a straight line.

Goat Sleeve
or
Lining Sleeve.

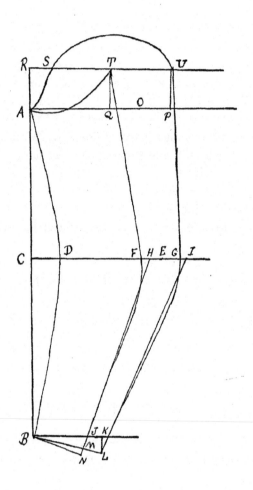

In cutting pattern allow ½ inch seams everywhere except on inside seam   One inch or more should be allowed here until after the sleeve has been fitted.   Gather top of sleeve from 1½ inches from A to U.

LESSON XVII

THE ONE-PIECE TIGHT SLEEVE

To make the one-piece tight sleeve, trace off on another piece of paper the upper piece of coat or lining sleeve.

Lay line T-F of the under piece on line U-G of the upper piece and trace the under piece. This makes a sleeve which fits exactly like the coat or lining sleeve, but it has no seam at the back from the elbow up. It is used for the lining of fancy sleeves and often for the outside Where one wishes to put tucks around the arm it will be found useful. It is good for the lining of sleeves made of thin material where the seam would not look well. It makes a fine lining for the mousquetaire sleeve.

One Piece Tight Sleeve

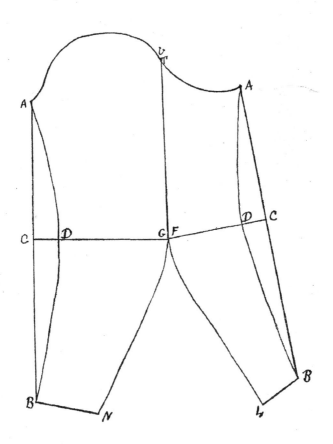

LESSON XVIII

THE FLOWING SLEEVE

THE flowing sleeve is made from the coat or lining sleeve as the one-piece sleeve was. Trace off on another piece of paper the upper sleeve. Lay line T-F of the under on line U-G of the upper and trace off the under piece of the sleeve.

1. Measure up from point B of the upper 4¼ inches. Mark this point F.

2. Measure from point N 4 inches. Mark this point E.

3. Draw a straight line through E and F and extend it 3 inches beyond F. Mark this point I.

4. Measure from L on the under piece up 4 inches. Mark this point G.

5. Measure from B up 4¼ inches. Mark this point H.

6. Draw a line through G and H and extend 3 inches beyond H. Mark this point J

7. Mark the point where these lines cross K.

8. Place point C on the chart at I and hold chart so that curve C-F touches line D-A   Draw curve.

9. Place point C on the chart at J and hold chart so that curve C-F touches line D-A. Draw curve.

10. Hold curve O-J on the chart so that it touches lines J-K and I-K. Draw curve.

In cutting pattern allow seams everywhere. The flowing sleeve is sometimes used in dresses but more often in dressing sacks and kimonos.

Flowing Sleeve.

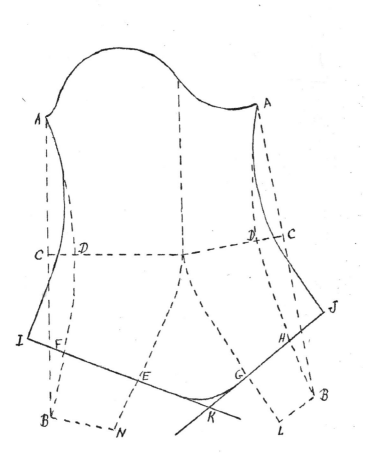

LESSON XIX

MEASURES used in draft given —

Arm Length	20 inches
Arm Length to bend of Elbow	9½ inches
Armhole measure	15 inches
Elbow measure	12½ inches
Hand measure	8 inches

1. Draw line A-B length of Arm measure

2. From A measure length of Arm to bend of Elbow. Mark this point C

3. At C square a line with line A-B.

4. From C on this line measure 2 inches. Mark this point D.

5. From D measure ½ of Elbow measure. Mark this point E.

6. Measure to the left of E 1¼ inches. Mark this point F.

7. Measure to the right of E 1¼ inches. Mark this point G.

8. Measure to the right of F ¼ inch. Mark this point H.

9. Measure to the right of G ¼ inch. Mark this point I.

10 Square a line at B with line A-B

11. On this line measure from B ½ of Hand measure. Mark this point J

12. To the right of J measure ¼ inch. Mark this point K.

13. At K square a line with line B-K.

14. Measure on this line from K 1 inch. Mark this point L.

15. Connect points L and B with a straight line

16. Measure on this line from L 1 inch. Mark this point M

17. Connect points M and H with a straight line, also points L and I

18. Place point D on the chart at point D and draw a curve to B.

19. Place point D on the chart at D and draw a curve to A.

20. Place point F on the chart at F and hold so that point J touches line H-M and draw curve.

21. Place point F on the chart at G and hold so that point J just touches line I-L and draw curve.

22. Measure line G-L and extend line F-M below M to make it the same length   Mark this point N.

23 Connect N and B with a straight line.

24. At A square a line with line A-B.

25. From A on this line measure ½ the Armhole measure. Mark this point O.

26. Measure to the right of O 4 times the distance from E to G   Mark this point P.

27. Measure to the left of O 2 inches   Mark this point Q.

28 Extend line A-B above A 2½ inches. Mark this point R

29 At R square a line with line R-B.

30 On this line measure from R 1½ inches   Mark this point S

31. Place point G on the chart at S and draw a curve through A.

32. At point Q square a line with line A-P. Mark the point T where this line touches the line from S.

33 At P square a line with line A-P and mark the point U where this line touches the line from S

34. Connect points F and T with a straight line.

35. Place point G on the chart at T and hold the chart so that the curve touches line A-P, draw curve and continue to A.

36. Measure 1 inch to the right of U. Mark this point V.

37 Place point D on the chart at G and draw curve towards V   Extend curve to V

38 Find a point on line R-V half way between S and V. Mark this point W.

Sleeve With Tight Elbow
and Large Top.

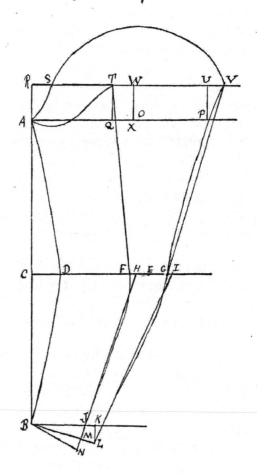

39. Square a line at W with line R-V and mark point **X** where this line touches A-P.

40 With X as a center and X-S as a radius, draw curve from S to V.

This completes the draft   If the sleeve is desired larger or smaller change the distance from O to P. The draft given, gives a medium sized sleeve

In cutting pattern allow seams everywhere.

LESSON XX

DRAFTING THE LEG O' MUTTON SLEEVE

MEASURES used in draft given —

Arm Length measure . .	20	inches
Arm Length to bend of Elbow	9½	inches
Armhole measure	15	inches
Elbow measure	12½	inches
Hand measure	8	inches

1. Draw line A-B length of Arm measure.

2. Measure from A length of Arm to bend of Elbow. Mark this point C.

3. At C square a line with line A-B.

4. On this line measure from C, 2 inches. Mark this point D.

5. From D measure ½ the Elbow measure. Mark this point E.

6. Measure to the left of E, 1¼ inches. Mark this point F.

7. Measure to the right of E, 2½ inches. Mark this point G.

8. Measure to the right of F, ¼ inch. Mark this point H.

9. Measure to the right of G, ¼ inch. Mark this point I.

10. At B square a line with line A-B.

11. On this line measure from B, ½ the Hand measure. Mark this point J.

12. Measure to the right of J, ¼ inch   Mark this point K

13. At K square a line with line B-K.

14. On this line measure from K, 1 inch. Mark this point L.

15. Connect L and B with a straight line.

16. Measure on this line from L, 1 inch. Mark this point M.

17. Connect points M and H with a straight line, also points L and I.

18. Place point D on the chart at D and draw a curve to point B.

19. Place point D on the chart at D and draw a curve to point A.

20. Place point F on the chart at F and hold chart so that point J touches line H-M. Draw curve

21 Place point F on the chart at G and hold chart so that point J touches line I-L   Draw curve

22. Measure line G-L and extend line F-M below M, to make it the length of G-L. Mark this point N

23. Connect N and B with a straight line.

24. At A square a line with line A-B.

25. From A on this line measure ½ the Armhole measure. Mark this point O.

26. Measure to the right of O twice the distance from E to G. Mark this point P.

27. Measure to the left of O, 2 inches. Mark this point Q.

28. Extend line A-B above A, 2½ inches. Mark this point R.

29. At R square a line with line R-B.

30 On this line measure from R, 1½ inches. Mark this point S.

31 Place point G on the chart at S, and draw curve through A.

32 At point Q square a line with line A-P. Mark the point T, where this line touches the line from S.

33. At P square a line with line A-P and mark the point U where this line touches the line from S.

34. Connect points F and T with a straight line.

35. Place point G on the chart at point T and hold chart so that the curve touches line A-P. Draw curve and continue it to A.

36. Measure 1 inch to the right of U. Mark this point V.

37. Draw a straight line from G to a point half way between U and V.

Leg O'Mutton Sleeve.

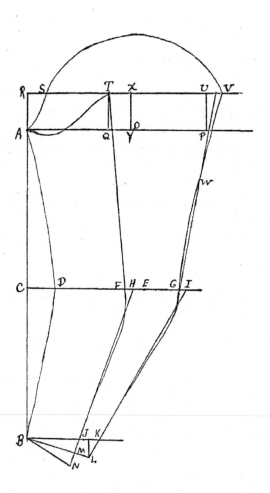

38 Find a point half way between V and G. Mark this point W.

39. Place point C on the chart at G, and hold chart so that point L falls on line from G.   Draw curve.

40 Place point D on the chart at V and let curve fall on W. Draw curve through W and V.

41 Find a point on a line R-V half way between S and V. Mark this X.

42 Square a line at X with line R-V, and mark point Y where this line touches line A-P.

43 With Y as a center and S-Y as a radius draw curve from S to V.

NOTE — To make the sleeve larger or smaller, change the distance from E to G, and from O to P. The draft given makes a medium sized sleeve.

In cutting pattern allow seams everywhere

LESSON XXI

TRACE off on another piece of paper the upper portion of the sleeve BE SURE TO TRACE ON THE LINE D-G, WHICH MARKS THE ELBOW.

Cut out, allowing seams everywhere except at the hand. One-half inch seam should be allowed at the top and outside seam. Allow at least 1 inch or more on the inside seam until after the sleeve has been fitted. It is at this seam that the sleeve should be changed if it needs any changing Sometimes you will find people with a very fully developed muscle between the shoulder and elbow. If this is so the sleeve will nearly always have to be let out at this point. Therefore leave seam enough to be able to let it out if needed. Now trace off the under portion of the sleeve, leaving the same sized seams. BE SURE TO TRACE ON LINE D-F. Now we are ready to cut the sleeve out of the lining goods. Always place the sleeve on the lining with the lines F-T and G-U on the straight of the goods lengthwise. Your lining, of course, is double fold, so that you will cut both sleeves at the same time BE SURE TO TRACE ON LINE D-F BEFORE YOU LIFT THE PATTERN. After all seams have been traced pick up the pattern. Make a notch at point U or V, whichever sleeve draft is being used, and one about 1½ inches from A. Pin the back seam together first. Begin by pinning the elbow line of the upper to the elbow line of the under and then pin the entire seam, being very careful to follow the tracing on each piece. After this seam is basted, pin the elbow lines of the outside seam together and baste in the same way as you did the inside seam. Gather the top from one notch to the other. The sleeve is ready to be fitted. This should be done at the time the waist lining is fitted, while the waist lining is on your patron. Pull up the gathers at the top and pin the sleeve to the armhole under the arm. Have your patron bend her arm and bring her arm forward at the shoulder to be sure the sleeve does not draw at the elbow If it should draw a little, see if the elbow is located just right and that you have not pinned it in too far to the waist in the back, at the back seam. After the sleeve is thoroughly fitted turn it up at the hand to just the right length. Before removing from your patron, mark where the front seam comes, on the waist. Remove the waist and sleeve from your patron and you are ready to proceed with the outside of the sleeve

If your sleeve is to be a plain one with the trimming placed on the outside, the outside goods will be cut just like the lining. If, however, the outside is to be very different, a pattern must be cut for the outside. There are sleeve forms which may be bought, like the bust forms. If one is going to work for others it always pays to have one of these forms The best way to learn to cut the fancy outside is to take an old piece of cloth. Cut what you think will make what you want and keep changing it until you get it just right. With a little practice, you can make just what you want the first time. Most sleeves conform quite closely to the lining, so you will not have much trouble. If there are to be tucks in the sleeve they must be put in the goods before it is cut out.

To make the Mousquetaire sleeve. This is the sleeve which is fulled on the lining from the shoulder to the hand. For this sleeve use the tight lining sleeve. Cut out the lining and sew up the elbow seam. Gather the goods on to the lining at the inside seam, allowing about once and a half the length of the sleeve. Be sure that the outside is the same size as the lining crosswise. Sew up the inside seam and tack the fullness to the lining all along the outside seam, or where it would be, so that it cannot drop down out of place. Be careful to make the fastenings so that they do not show. When large sleeves are being worn, a very pretty sleeve is made by putting small length-

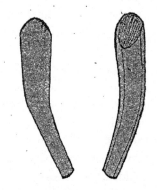

Coat Sleeve
or
Lining Sleeve

Leg O' Mutton
Sleeve

Flowing Sleeve

wise tucks from the hand to the elbow, allowing the sleeve to puff from the elbow to the shoulder. In cutting this sleeve the tucks must be placed in the goods and all the fullness left by the tucks must be left in the sleeve. For this sleeve use the one-piece lining After sewing up the outside seam to the elbow, fasten the tucks in place on the lining. Baste the goods on the lining. Cut out the sleeve and baste up. Gather the outside at the top in to the size of the lining, and then gather both the lining and outside in to the size of the armhole A little of the fullness left by the tucks may be shoved off at the sides but not enough to make it look drawn at the top of the tucks. A bias band or a fancy shaped cuff may be placed at the hand or it may be simply faced with a bias facing If you wish a sleeve to be sewed in at the armhole without gathers, take the sleeve off at the highest part of the top about 1 inch, and take it in enough at point A to make it the exact size of the armhole. The one-piece sleeve is the best one to use for this sleeve.

After the sleeve is all stitched and pressed, lay it away with the waist until the skirt and drop skirt are prepared All that is left to do to the sleeve is to face it about the hand with a bias facing, of silk if the goods is very heavy; if not, of the goods itself.

LESSON XXII

DRAFTING THE CIRCULAR SKIRT

MEASURES used for draft given —

Waist measure	25 inches
Hip measure	42 inches
Front length of skirt	40 inches
Side length of skirt	40½ inches
Back length of skirt	41½ inches

Take a sheet of paper having a square corner and one straight edge large enough for the draft. If a piece large enough is not at hand, paste several together.

1. Use the corner of the paper for a center, and a radius of 10 inches, and draw a circle. Point A.

2. With the same center and a radius of 15 inches, draw another circle   Point C.

3. Measure from A on circle, ½ the Waist measure. Mark this point B

4. Measure from C on circle, ½ the Hip measure. Mark this point D.

5. Find a point on circle A-B half way between A and B. Mark this point E.

6. Measure down ¾ of an inch from B. Mark this point F.

7 Place point J on the chart at E, and with curve J-F draw curve towards F. Continue curve to F.

8. Find a point on circle C-D half way between C and D. Mark this point G.

9. Measure down from D ¾ of an inch. Mark this point H.

Circular Skirt.

Circular Skirt.

Edge of Paper
Back of Skirt.
B F D H
waistline
line
Hip line
A
E
G
C
J
L
Edge of Paper
Front line
Bottom Line of Skirt.
M
K

10. Place point J on the chart at G and with curve J-F draw curve towards H. Continue curve to H.

11. Measure from A on circle A-F ½ of Waist measure. Mark this point I.

12. Measure from C on circle C-H, ½ of Hip measure. Mark this point J.

13. Draw a straight line through I and J and continue down the length of the Back skirt measure This line is the center back line.

14. Measure from A down the edge of the paper, which is the front center line of the skirt, the Front length measure of the skirt. Point K

15. Measure down from I the Back length of skirt Point L.

16. Measure from E the Side length of skirt Point M.

17. The curve for the bottom of the skirt is found by measuring down every few inches the length measures of the skirt

This skirt draft should never be used for narrow goods. It should always be cut from very heavy goods

In cutting pattern allow seams down the back and at the waist line.

LESSON XXIII

MEASURES used in draft given —

Waist measure	25 inches
Hip measure	42 inches
Front Length measure	40 inches
Side Length measure	40½ inches
Back Length measure	41½ inches

Take a sheet of paper having a square corner and one straight edge large enough to hold the draft.

1. Use the corner of the paper for a center and with a radius of 10 inches draw a circle. Point A

2 With the same center and a radius of 15 inches draw another circle. Point C.

3. Measure from A on circle, ½ of Waist measure. Mark this point B.

4. Measure from C on circle, ½ of Hip measure. Mark this point D.

5. Find a point on circle A-B half way between A and B. Mark this point E.

6. Measure down ¾ of an inch from B. Mark this point F.

7 Place point J on the chart at E and with curve J-F draw curve towards F. Continue curve to F.

8. Find a point on circle C-D half way between C and D and mark this point G.

9. Measure down from D ¾ of an inch. Mark this point H.

10. Place point J on the chart at G and with curve J-F draw curve towards H. Continue curve to H.

109

Three Gored

Circular Skirt.

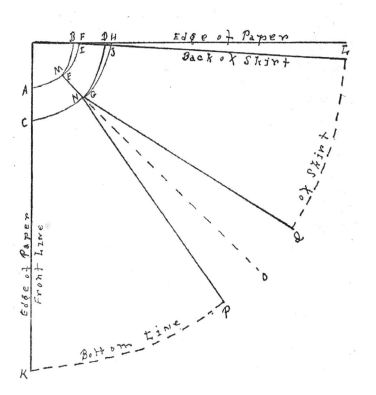

11. Measure from A on circle A-F, ½ of Waist measure. Mark this point I.

12. Measure from C on circle C-H, ½ of Hip measure. Mark this point J.

13. Draw a straight line through I-J and continue down the length of the Back skirt measure   This line is the center back line.

14   Measure from A down the edge of the paper, which is the front center line of the skirt, the Front skirt length   Point K.

15. Measure down from I the back length of skirt.   Point L

16. On circle A-F measure 1 inch to the left of point E   Mark this point M.

17. On circle C-H measure 1 inch to the left of G.   Mark this point N.

18. Draw a line through M and N and continue down the length of Side skirt measure.   Mark this point O.

19. Measure to the right and left of O on the bottom curve of skirt, 9 inches   Mark these points P and Q.

20. Connect N and P, and N and Q with straight lines.

21. A-K-M-P is the front gore   M-Q-I-L is the back gore. In cutting out the pattern allow seams everywhere.

NOTE — The three-gored circular skirt draft is the same as the full circular skirt, except that a half-yard is taken out at the sides   This gives less fullness, and the seam down the side keeps the skirt from sagging.

LESSON XXIV

DRAFTING THE SEVEN-GORED SKIRT

MEASURES used in this draft —

Waist measure	25 inches
Hip measure .	42 inches
Front length of skirt	40 inches
Side length of skirt .	40½ inches
Back length of skirt	41½ inches
Measure about bottom .	3 yards

Take a piece of paper having one square corner and a straight edge, large enough to hold the draft.

1. A represents the corner of the paper

2. With A as a center and a radius of 10 inches, draw a circle B-D, beginning at the edge of the paper, A-P.

3. With A as a center and a radius of 15 inches, draw another circle, C-E.

4. From C on circle C-E, measure 1-7 of one half the Hip measure   Mark this point F

5   From point C on circle C-E measure 1½ inches more than from C to F.   Mark this point G

6. Measure from C to F and C to G   Subtract this amount from ½ the Hip measure

7. Use what is left of the Hip measure for the distance from C to H and C to I, making C to H ½ inch less than C to I.

8. From B on circle B-D measure 1 inch less than from C to F. Mark this point K.

9   From B on circle B-D measure ¾ inch more than from B to K.   Mark this point L.

10. Measure from B to K and B to L and subtract this sum from ½ the Waist measure.

11. Use what is left of the Waist measure for the distance from B to M and B to N, making B to M ½ inch less than B to N.

12. Place point C on the chart at point F and draw curve through K.

13 Place point D on the chart at G and draw curve through L.

14. Place point D on the chart at H and draw curve through M.

15 Place point D on the chart at I and draw curve through N.

16 To form the inverted plait — Measure on a straight line from G, touching the circle C-E, 4 inches   Mark this point J.

17. From L measure on a straight line touching the circle B-D, 3½ inches   Mark this point O.

18. Measure up from O, ¾ of an inch   Mark this point OO.

19. Place point F on the chart at OO and draw curve through L.

20. Connect OO and J with a straight line.

21. To form the bottom of the gores — Measure down from B on the edge of the paper the Front length of skirt.   Mark this point P.

22. With A as a center and A-P as a radius, draw a circle, beginning at the edge of the paper   Circle P-V.

23. From P on circle P-V measure 3½ inches more than from C to F   Mark this point Q

24. Decide how wide you wish your skirt about the bottom. This will be determined by the style being worn.

25 Subtract from ½ the bottom measure the distance from P to Q

26 Divide what is left of the bottom measure into three equal parts   Use one of these parts as a measure for the three other gores.

27. Make the distance from P to R 2 inches less than this 1-3 measure.

28. Now find out how much of the ½ bottom measure you

Seven Gored Skirt

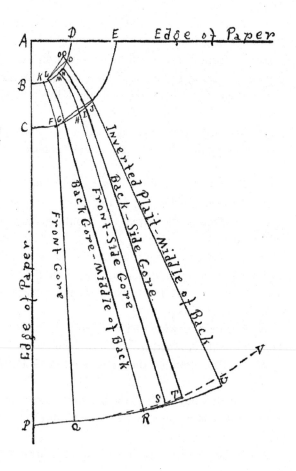

have used, by measuring from P to Q and from P to R. Subtract this sum from $\frac{1}{2}$ the bottom measure.

29   Divide what is left into two equal parts   Use this measure for the two side gores, making P to S 2 inches less than P to T.

30. Measure from point R, 10 inches, point U, for the bottom of inverted plait

31. Connect with straight lines points F and Q, G and R, H and S, I and T, J and U

32   To find the true bottom curve of each gore, measure down from waist curve, on each line, the skirt lengths.

33. The front gore is represented by B-P-K-Q.

34. The back gore is represented by B-P-L-R, with inverted plait L-R-O-U

35   Front Side Gore is represented by B-P-M-S.

36. Back Side Gore is represented by B-P-N-T.

37   To lay the inverted plait, place line L-R over on line O-U.

In putting the skirt together the straight side of each gore B-P will come against the bias side of the gore next to it.

In cutting the pattern allow seams everywhere.

LESSON XXV

DRAFTING THE NINE-GORED SKIRT

MEASURES used for draft given —

Waist measure	. 25	inches
Hip measure . ..	 42	inches
Front Length measure .. .	40	inches
Side Length measure	40½	inches
Back Length measure .	41½	inches
Measure about bottom .	3	yards

Take a piece of paper having a square corner and one straight side.

1. A represents the corner.

2. With A as a center and a radius of 10 inches, draw a circle, B-D.

3. With A as a center and 15 inches as a radius, draw a circle, C-E.

4. From C on circle C-E measure 1-9 of half the Hip measure. Mark this point F.

5. From B on circle B-D measure ¾ inch less than from C to F. Mark this point I.

6 Measure down from B the skirt length measure. Mark this point M.

7. From M, measure 3½ inches more than from C to F. Mark this point N.

8. Connect I and F, and F and N with straight lines This forms the front gore

9. From ½ the Hip measure subtract the distance from C to F.

10. Divide what is left into 4 equal parts. This gives the

Nine Gored Skirt.

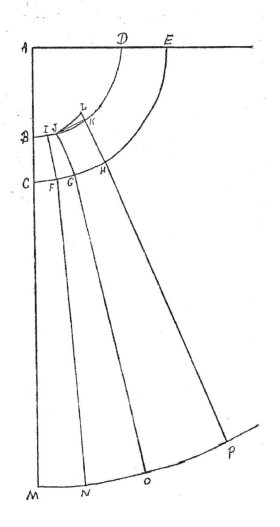

Hip measure for each of the other gores, or the distance from C to G.

11. Subtract from ½ the Waist measure the distance from B to I.

12. Divide what is left into 4 equal parts. This gives the measure for the waist line of all the other gores, or distance from B to J.

13. Subtract from ½ the bottom measure the distance from M to N.

14. Divide what is left into 4 equal parts. This gives the measure for the bottom of all the gores, or the distance from M to O.

15. After cutting the front gore, B-M-I-N, cut 6 gores like the gore represented by B-M-J-O

16. To make the back gores — Add the inverted plait

17. Measure from G on a straight line touching curve C-H, 3½ inches. Mark this point H.

18. Measure from J on a straight line touching curve C-E, 3½ inches. Mark this point K.

19. Measure on a straight line from O, 10 inches. Mark this point P.

20 Measure up from K, ½ inch. Mark this point L. Place point F on the chart at L, and draw curve through J.

21 Connect L and H, and H and P with straight lines.

22. B-M-L-P represents the back gore with inverted plait. Cut two of these gores. You will have 9 gores in all

Notch each gore as it is cut out, to show just where each one goes. Always put the straight side B-M against the bias side of the next gore. Get the true bottom curve as you did the seven-gored skirt. To lay inverted plait, place line J-O on line L-P.

In cutting pattern allow seams everywhere.

LESSON XXVI

DRAFTING THE FIFTEEN-GORED SKIRT

MEASURES used for draft given —

Waist measure	25	inches
Hip measure	42	inches
Front Length measure	40	inches
Side Length measure	40½	inches
Back Length measure	41½	inches
Measure about bottom	3	yards

Take a piece of paper having a square corner and one straight edge.

1. A represents the corner.

2. With A as a center and a radius of 10 inches, draw a circle, beginning at the straight edge of the paper (B-C).

3. With the same center and a radius of 15 inches, draw another circle (D-E).

4. From D on circle D-E measure 1-15 of the Hip measure. Mark this point F.

5. From B on circle B-C measure 1-15 of the Waist measure. Mark this point G.

6 From B on the edge of the paper measure down the Front skirt length. Mark this point H

7. From H measure 2 inches more than from D to F   Mark this point I.

8. Place point C on the chart at F and draw curve through G.

9. Connect F and I with a straight line. This forms the front gore.

10 Subtract from ½ the Hip measure, the distance from D to F.

Fifteen Gored Skirt.

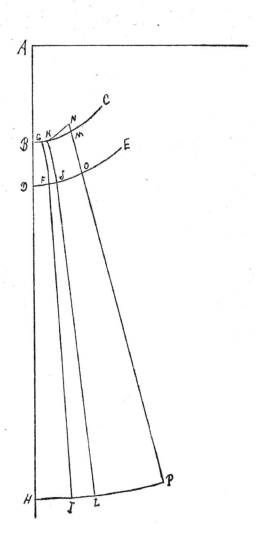

11. Divide what is left into 7 equal parts.

12. Measure from D on circle D-E one of these parts. Mark this point J.

13. Subtract from ½ the Waist measure the distance from B to G.

14. Divide what is left into 7 equal parts.

15. Measure from B on circle B-C one of these parts. Mark this point K.

16. Place point D on the chart at J and draw curve through K.

17. Connect J and L with a straight line. This finishes the side gore. Twelve of these should be cut.

18. To form the back gore — Add to the side gore the inverted plait.

19. Measure on a straight line from K touching the curve, 2½ inches Mark this point M.

20 Measure up from M ½ inch. Mark this point N.

21. Measure from J on a straight line touching curve, 3 inches. Mark this point O.

22. Measure from L, 8 inches. Mark this point P.

23. Connect N-O and P with a straight line.

The entire back gore is represented by B-H-N-P.

The side gores by B-H-K-L.

The front gore by B-H-G-I

To lay the inverted plait, lay line L-K over on line N-P.

In cutting pattern allow all seams.

LESSON XXVII

FOR this skirt make the bottom measure 2½ yards, when you make your draft.

1 Trace off on another piece of paper the front gore.

2. Measure out 1 inch from G.

3. Measure out 1¼ inches from F.

4 Measure out 2½ inches from I.

5 Connect these two points with straight lines, and cut on this line   This amount added to the gore is for the plait.

6. Turn the plait under, turning on line G-F-I.

7 Trace off the side gore.

8 Measure out from B, 1 inch

9 Measure out from D, 1¼ inches.

10. Measure out from H, 2½ inches.

11. Connect these points with straight lines.

This amount added is for a lap to run under the plait of the front gore

12. Measure out from K, 1 inch

13. Measure out from J, 1¼ inches.

14 Measure out from L, 2½ inches.

This forms the plait to be turned under on the side gore. This forms the entire skirt except the two back gores

15 To form the back gores — Trace off the back gore, having added the inverted plait.

16. Measure out from B, 1 inch

17. Measure out from D, 1¼ inches.

18 Measure out from H, 2½ inches.

19. Connect these points with straight lines.   This forms

Full Plaited Skirt.

Fifteen Gore.

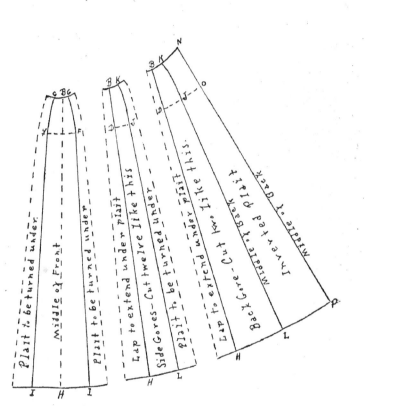

the lap to run under the plait of the gore next to the back. Lay the inverted plait by placing line K-J-L over on N-O-P.

Cut the same number of gores of each kind as directed in the plain fifteen-gored skirt.

In cutting from the goods, the line marked B-H on the illustration must be marked with a thread before the pattern is raised from the goods After each plait has been turned in, baste it flat to the next gore. Have the edge of the plait follow the line B-H each time. Stitch on the edge of each plait from the waist down about 10 inches. Turn the skirt wrong side out and stitch the raw edge of the plaits to the raw edge of the laps in a flat seam about ½ inch wide. Before removing the bastings which hold the plaits in place, give each plait a dead press by placing a wet cloth on it and pressing until dry. Use a rather heavy iron. The skirt should be placed on a band at the waist and hung about the bottom, before removing the bastings. After the skirt is hung even about the bottom, run a thread where it is to turn up and then remove the bastings. Turn up the hem and stitch it in. Press the hem and then press the plaits back in where they were pressed out in pressing the hem.

LESSON XXVIII

FIRST we will take up the drop skirt. The amount of material for the drop skirt must depend on the style of the outside skirt. If the skirts worn are very scant the drop skirt must be made to correspond. If very full, it must be made with a full ruffle or plaiting. Five and one half yards of cotton lining or 10 yards of taffeta will make a full drop skirt.

You have of course decided whether your outside skirt is to be scant or full and we take it for granted that you have drafted your pattern.

You should do all the drafting before you begin the gown, waist, sleeve and skirt.

Use the draft you have made for the skirt. Trace off each gore on another piece of paper and allow seams everywhere. Of course a seam will not be allowed down the front of the draft, as only ½ the front is drafted   Allow ½ inch seam at the waist line and ¾ inch on all sides of the gores. The pattern should be made just the length the skirt is to be when finished. In using the seven-gored skirt, if the skirts worn are a little full, slant the lines from the hips down out a little. If they are worn very tight, draw the lines just a little slanting   Notch each gore as it is cut from the paper, beginning with the front, which has one notch. The side of the second gore which comes next to the front has one notch, and the other side of this gore two notches. So on until all the gores are notched.

Turn each gore up 10 inches from the bottom and pin   Use this for a pattern for the drop skirt. Spread the lining out on the table. It will be double fold, if cotton   Lay the middle of the front gore on the lengthwise fold of the goods and arrange the other gores to the best advantage to save cloth. The goods being plain, the gores may be turned either way up or down. Cut out, allowing a good seam at the bottom, as we are to sew our ruffle or plaiting to it Notch each gore to correspond to those in the pattern Baste all the seams and stitch

From the other end of the goods, cut enough strips $11\frac{1}{4}$ inches wide, on a true bias, to make, when sewed together end to end, once and a half the width of the skirt around the bottom. Sew the seams on the machine. Turn and baste a hem $1\frac{1}{2}$ inches wide along one side Gather along the other side about $\frac{1}{2}$ inch from the edge. Before gathering, divide into quarters and gather each quarter on a separate thread. Divide the bottom of the skirt into four parts, making the two front parts two inches more than the back parts This will bring the ruffle a little fuller in the back than in front. Sew the ruffle to the skirt, having the seam come on the wrong side Have the seam on the skirt as wide again as that on the ruffle After the skirt has been tried on, turn the wide part of the seam over the narrow part, turning in, and stitch. This covers all the raw edge where the ruffle is put on A narrow ruffle may be put on the wide one at the bottom if one wishes. If a plaiting is preferred in place of the ruffle, enough strips should be cut on the straight of the goods, the same width as those for the ruffle, to make 3 times the width of the skirt.

Sew a straight band of the goods about $1\frac{1}{2}$ inches wide to the top of the skirt, having the band about 2 inches longer than the waist measure. Pin the middle of the band to the middle of the front of the skirt, having the band on the right side of the skirt. Turn in both ends of the band 1 inch and pin along the top of the skirt. You will find that the skirt is quite a bit longer than the band. What is left of the skirt may be gathered in, or laid in a large plait, having the edge of the plait come just to the end of the band

The back seam of the skirt should be left open about 12 inches from the top This opening should be hemmed on each side with a narrow hem. A silk drop skirt is cut the same except that there is no fold to cut the front gore on Fold the goods together to cut the front, and proceed as in the cotton skirt

The Outside Skirt — Turn the bottom of the pattern down again, where you turned it up to use it for the drop skirt. This leaves the pattern just the length the finished skirt is to be. We will make a perfectly plain skirt Spread the goods on the table, if possible wrong side up. Never cut the front gore of the outside skirt on the fold that is in the goods, if it is double-fold goods. This used always to be done, but it is no longer considered proper. Make a fresh fold just far enough from the edge of the goods to cut the gore After this gore is cut, lay all others on, to the best advantage possible NEVER lay the front side of the gores exactly on the straight of the goods lengthwise. Always lay the top of the gore back at least 1½ inches. Always allow about 4 inches at the bottom of each gore for hem If you are short of goods only allow two inches, and then the skirt may be faced. It is never best to cut a skirt the exact length it is to be, for it always takes up in making. Before raising the pattern from the goods, turn back all seams on the pattern and mark on the goods with tailor's chalk Also mark where the bottom of the pattern comes on each gore Be sure to notch each gore to correspond with the pattern. Pin the front gore to the second ones, one at a time, and baste. Pin every few inches and be careful not to stretch either side. When all the seams have been basted in this way, turn the skirt up about the bottom, on the wrong side, on the line you made with the chalk. The chalk rubs off easily so it is best to trace on the line with thread before handling the skirt. Pin every few inches and high enough up so that the hem will not drop down. Run a strong thread along the waist line to keep it from stretching when it is tried on.

We are ready now for the first fitting. When the patron comes, if the waist and skirt are to be separate, put the skirt on first, over the drop skirt. Examine very carefully to see if it is a perfect fit about the hips and waist and notice whether the seams all look straight. Do not try to hang the skirt around the bottom until the seams are stitched and pressed. While the skirt is on the patron lay the inverted plait in the back, if there is to be one. Nowadays there are so many different styles of skirts, that you will have to use your ingenuity Some open on the side, some at the side of the back and some at the side of the front. All we can do is to tell you how to make the plain skirt. After the skirt is thoroughly fitted, put on the waist. Be sure the outside looks just as it should when finished Make any changes necessary. Pin the sleeve into the armhole, taking care that the inside seam comes just where it should to hang right. Cut a collar just as you were taught to cut the neck band for the shirt waist, only wider, of whatever material the collar is to be and 1 inch wider than when finished. Pin it in place on the patron, shape the top and get the exact length. Remove the gown carefully so as not to lose any pins, and it is ready to finish. There should be one more fitting, after the gown is all finished except the hem in the bottom. If you do this your work will never have to be brought back for changes Finish up the drop skirt, which, if it needs no changes, is all finished but sewing on the band. Turn down the edge of the band, which is not basted, and baste on the wrong side just opposite the first basting. Stitch on the right side. This will make a band about $\frac{1}{2}$ inch wide at the top of the skirt Sew a good large hook and eye on the band and press the entire skirt This finishes the drop skirt Finish up the waist according to the style it is to be. If a separate waist is worn outside the skirt, the bottom of the waist should be finished with a bias band about $1\frac{1}{2}$ inches wide. Stitch the band on the right side, turn up on the wrong side and hem. Stitch it the first time just a seam below the ends of the bones, so that when it is finished the bones will come clear to the bottom of the waist. Finish all other parts neatly and fasten all trimmings where they should be. Baste in the sleeves and stitch. Bind the armholes with a bias band wide enough to cover the seam Finish the sleeves at the bottom with a hem or facing. Place No. 1 hooks and Peet or thread loops, whichever seem best, wherever necessary.

After the waist is all finished we must finish the skirt. Stitch all seams. If the skirt has been fastened to the waist, this is hard to do, but it can be accomplished. Turn the skirt wrong side out. Cut a stitch at the waist line near the seam and fasten with a pin so that it cannot ravel but so you can get at the seam. Stitch all seams Trim off to about ½ inch, and overcast. Press open. If the skirt is separate from the waist we must put a band on at the waist line, just as we did on the drop skirt. A waist band may be bought ready made or one may be made as we did for the drop skirt. It is best if you are sewing for others to buy the ready made band. Before putting on this band, the placket should be finished. Put a facing about 1½ inches wide down the left side of the placket, made of goods like the skirt, and perfectly straight of the goods lengthwise. Stitch on the right side, turn on the wrong side and hem. To the other side of the placket, sew a straight piece of the goods, 4 inches wide, which has been folded together lengthwise. Sew one edge to the unfinished side of the placket, having the piece on the right side of the skirt. Turn in the other edge, baste along the stitching just made and stitch again on the right side. Be sure to catch the last basting. This will form a flap 2 inches wide to run under the hem on the other side of the placket. You laid your inverted plait so that the edge of the plait came just to the edge of the placket. Stitch each plait in place on the machine about ¼ inch back from the edge. Place hooks on the hem side and Peet eyes on the flap. Now sew the band to the top of the skirt, and it is finished, all but the hem in the bottom. If the skirt is fastened to the waist the placket is finished in the same way.

The skirt we have given is a perfectly plain skirt If a fancy one is to be made, the pattern must be prepared before it is cut from the goods. If you wish a skirt with a circular flounce, pin all the gores together and cut a piece from the bottom of the skirt just the width you wish your flounce   Slash this piece up from the bottom every few inches   Spread each cut apart a little and paste a piece of paper underneath, to hold them apart. These slashes must extend almost to the top of the piece.   When all these slashes have been spread apart you will have your circular flounce.   Use the top of the pattern for the pattern of the skirt, allowing a little on the bottom to run under the flounce until it is properly hung   Allow a hem on the bottom of the flounce and a seam at the top.   Turn in the top and lay it flat on the skirt   Stitch on the outside as near the edge as possible. If you wish a fancy-shaped yoke in the skirt, pin the seams of the skirt together at the hips and waist line and cut a yoke any shape you wish.   Use the lower part of the pattern to cut the skirt by.   Turn in the lower edge of the yoke.   Place the skirt underneath and stitch as near the edge as possible   If a skirt is desired with set-in plaits half way up on some of the gores, decide how far up you wish them to come.   Cut these gores off where you wish the top of the plaits to come   Allow a hem on these gores about 2 inches wide.   Lay the plaits in a piece of paper, and pin them to the gore just where you want them. The top of the plaits must extend up under the hem far enough to catch when the hem is stitched in   Now cut the gore the same shape it was before.   This gives you an exact pattern for the gore with the plaits set in   Whenever any plaits are put in a skirt, always keep them securely basted in until the skirt is finished

You will soon learn to cut any kind of a skirt you wish.   Always begin with the plain foundation and work out your pattern from that

LESSON XXIX

For the petticoat to be placed on a band, use the draft given for the seven-gored skirt   Pin the front gore to the second, and cut together as one gore   This will make a wide front gore. The dart at the top where the front gore rounds in to the waist should be put in. Cut the back side gore just as it is   Cut the back gore without the inverted plait   Add 3 inches to the back seam at the top but not at the bottom   This will straighten the back seam and leave a few gathers at the waist in the back. Make the skirt a little less around the bottom than you would make an outside skirt. If very full dress skirts are being worn, a 3-yard skirt will be found a good width for a petticoat. The width must depend on the dress skirts being worn. Cut the skirt as much shorter than it is to be as the width of embroidery edge, lace or ruffle of the goods you wish to put on the bottom   This should be about 3 inches   Sew this ruffle (which should not be very full, less than once and a half the width of the skirt) to the bottom of the skirt, having the seam on the inside. Before stitching the ruffle on, place a straight band 2½ inches wide so that the edge comes just even with the edge of the ruffle where it is to be stitched on. Turn this band up on the skirt, having turned in the raw edge, and stitch in place   This covers the seam and forms the hem of the skirt.

Make a flounce from 8 to 12 inches wide of embroidery, or of muslin with embroidery or lace sewed on the edge. This flounce should measure once and a half the width of the skirt. Put the flounce on the bottom of the skirt, so that the lower edge of the flounce comes just even with the lower edge of the narrow ruffle which forms the bottom of the skirt. Place a narrow bias band about 3-8 of an inch wide, after both edges are turned in, over the seam where the flounce is sewed to the skirt   Stitch on both edges of this band very near the edge.

Leave the back seam of the skirt open for about 12 inches from the top. Hem the right side of this opening with a hem ½ inch wide and the left side with a narrow hem   Lap the right side over on the left at the bottom of the opening and stitch across on the machine so that it cannot tear down. Now gather the the skirt from the back side seam to the opening. Take a straight piece of muslin 2 inches wide, lengthwise of the goods, and 2 inches longer than the waist measure. Turn in each end 1 inch and turn in the raw edges. Fold together lengthwise so that the edges are just even. Sew to the top of the skirt, having one edge of the band on the right side of the skirt and the other on the wrong side. Stitch into place and work a buttonhole in the right hand end of the band and place a button on the left hand end. This finishes the skirt

The Petticoat with a Yoke. — Cut a yoke of the muslin, according to the directions for cutting yokes in LESSON 28, having made a pattern first. Make the yoke the same width from the waist line all the way around. Use the same foundation pattern you used for the petticoat just given, but add 6 inches at the back where the skirt is to sew on the yoke. This will make the back seam about straight, as we add nothing at the bottom. Of course the skirt will be cut as much shorter as the yoke is deep, this amount being taken off at the top and not at the bottom of the skirt. Gather the top of the skirt from back side seam to placket and sew to the bottom of the yoke, having the seam on the inside. Cover the seam with a narrow bias band. For this skirt the opening in the back must be faced instead of hemmed. Face with a straight piece of goods about 1½ inches wide   Lay one side over on the other at the bottom and stitch across as in the other skirt. This opening should be 12 inches long. Instead of the straight band at the waist line, stitch a bias band about 1 inch wide to the yoke at the waist

Seven Gored Skirt

Used for a Petticoat.

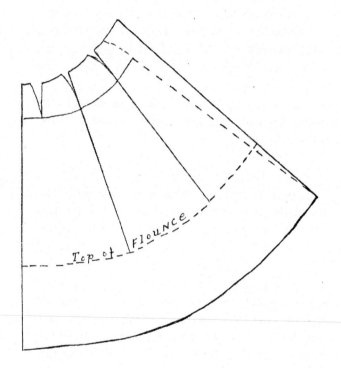

Top of Flounce

line, having the band on the right side of the skirt. Turn the
band over on the wrong side. Turn in the raw edge and stitch
again, as near the edge as possible   Stitch again near the top
edge of the skirt. Work a buttonhole and sew on a button near
the top of the yoke. Finish the skirt at the bottom the same as
the one given before.

LESSON XXX

THE NIGHT - GOWN

For the night-gown the shirt-waist draft is used. After deciding how deep the yoke is to be, trace off the pattern on a piece of paper, using the neck, shoulder and as much of the arm-hole as needed. For the skirt of the night-gown use the rest of the armhole which was not used in the yoke. For the under arm seam draw slanting lines from point T so that the skirt will be about 2 1-8 or 2¼ yards around the bottom. Allow a two-inch hem at the bottom of the gown, and at the front, where the skirt gathers on the yoke, 4 inches for gathers and 3 inches at the back. Gather the skirt to the yoke, having the seam on the right side, and cover the seam with finishing braid, which can be bought at any dry goods store The yoke may be made any depth, and as fancy as one wishes, using tucks, lace or embroidery. A very pretty gown may be made by using all-over embroidery for the yoke. The yoke may be buttoned down the front from the neck, or it may be cut away, leaving a V-shaped opening in front. There should be no seam down the front or back of the gown. If the goods is not wide enough to cut it, put gores on at the sides to make it wide enough. Open the skirt of the gown from the yoke down the front about 18 inches Put hem ¾ of an inch wide down the right side and a narrow hem down the left side of the opening. At the lower end lay the right side over on the left and stitch across to keep it from tearing down. For the sleeve use the shirt-waist draft. Gather the bottom into a band, or use a narrow band and sew a ruffle of lace or embroidery to the lower edge. The sleeve may be cut off short, the lower edge trimmed and left to hang loose.

Nightgown Made From Shirt-waist Draft.

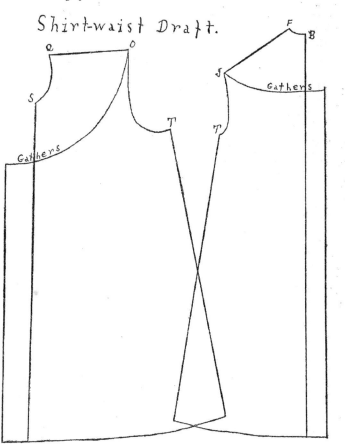

LESSON XXXI

THE CHEMISE

FOR the chemise the shirt-waist draft may also be used. Trace off on another piece of paper the neck, shoulder and armhole of the shirt-waist front. After this pattern has been made, trace with the tracing-wheel a circle extending from about 4 inches from the neck, on the front line, to a point about 2 inches from the armhole on the shoulder. Cut on this line and use the lower part for the pattern of the chemise Add 5 inches to the front of the pattern and draw a line from T 30 inches long, slanting out enough at the bottom to make the skirt measure ½ yard from the front line to the line just drawn. Make the front line long enough to correspond with the under arm line. For the back, trace off the neck, shoulder and armhole as you did for the front. Draw a circle from a point 2 inches from the armhole on the shoulder seam to a point 5 inches from the neck on the back line. Cut on this line and use the lower part of the pattern for the chemise. Add 5 inches to the back of the pattern and draw a line from T 30 inches long, slanting out enough to make the skirt measure ½ yard from the middle back seam to the line just drawn This makes the bottom of the finished garment measure 2 yards. The line down the back should slant out 2 or 3 inches, as shown in the drawing. To cut from the goods, lay the middle of the front and the middle of the back on the fold of the goods lengthwise. Cut a band 1¼ inches wide, the same circle as the neck of the chemise, leaving off the amount added for gathers. Join the front and back bands at the shoulders. Make this band double of the goods. Stitch the two pieces together at the upper edge and turn. Turn in both edges at the lower edge of the band about ¼ inch. Gather the chemise be-

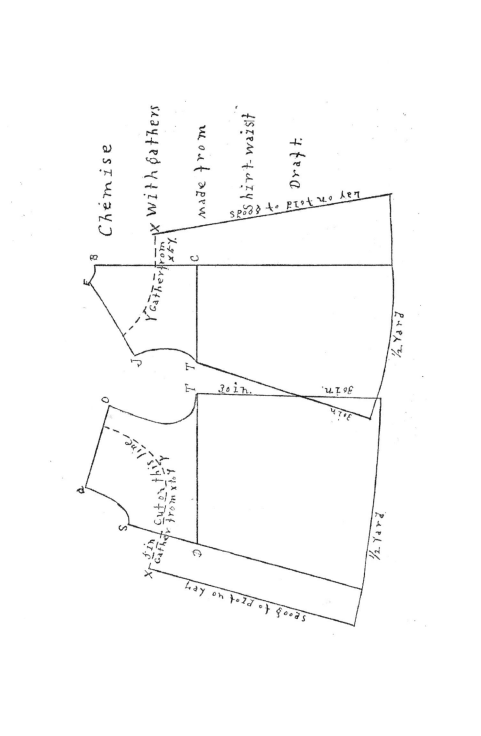

Chemise

X with gathers

made from

shirt-waist Draft.

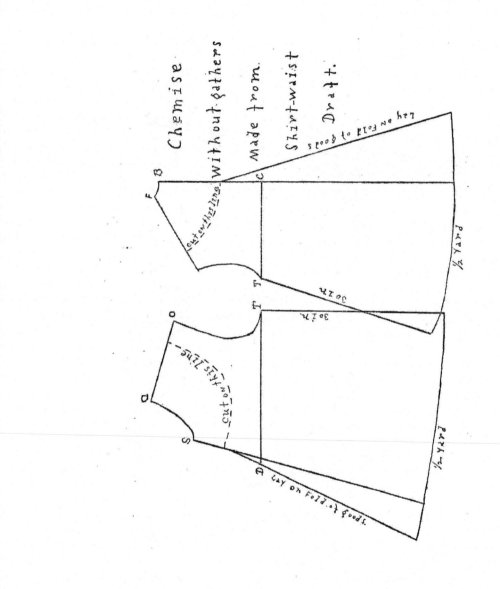

Chemise

Without Gathers

Made from

Shirt-waist

Draft.

B

F

cut on this line

C

lay on Fold of goods

½ Yard

T T

30 in.

30 in.

o

a

Cut on this line

S

A lay on Fold of goods

½ Yard

½ Yard

tween points X and Y into this band, placing one edge on the right and one on the wrong side. Stitch in place, as near the edge as possible Face the armhole with a bias facing cut 1 inch wide Sew this facing to the garment on the right side. Turn back on the wrong side and after turning in the raw edge stitch in place, stitching as near the edge as possible. Sew about the neck and armholes a narrow lace, fulled on. These chemise may be made very fancy, if one wishes, by putting in little yokes of insertion or embroidery.

The Chemise without Gathers. — Another way these garments are often made is without any gathers at the neck To cut one this way, simply do not add the 5 inches to the front and back, but draw the front and back lines slanting out 5 inches at the bottom. (See Ill.) This will take out the fullness at the yoke but will not narrow up the skirt. The chemise made this way is often embroidered in scallops about the neck and armholes.

LESSON XXXII

WOMEN'S CORSET COVERS

FOR the tight-fitting corset cover, use the tight waist draft without back forms Cut the pattern from paper, allowing seams everywhere. Cut the neck out as low as desired. In making this corset cover, sew up the seams on the wrong side, and after it has been fitted trim off one side of the seam, leaving it about ¼ inch wide Turn in the edge of the other side of the seam and baste down flat over the trimmed edge. (Fell seam.) Stitch as near the edge as possible. The seams should all be turned towards the back. A hem 1¼ inches wide should be made down each side of the front. Turn down this hem, having turned in the raw edge, and stitch. Sew buttons on the left hand hem and work buttonholes on the right hem. Trim the neck and armholes with lace or embroidery It makes the corset cover stronger to face the armholes and neck with a narrow bias binding, instead of just hemming them with a narrow hem.

Corset Cover Fulled at Neck and Waist Line. — Use the shirt-waist draft Cut out the neck as much as desired Add 3 inches on the front and nothing on the back. Do not add anything to the bottom of the waist. Hem the neck and armholes with a narrow hem and sew on beading and lace edge. Run a ribbon through the beading Gather the waist in at the bottom of the waist, beginning at about 5 inches from the under arm seam on the front and about 2 inches from this seam on the back. Sew to the bottom of the waist a circular piece of muslin. To draft this piece, take a radius of 12 inches and draw a part of a circle just ½ of the waist measure. Measure from this circle 3 inches. Draw another arc Slant the end out just a little. Cut from the cloth, laying the straight end on the fold of the

Corset Cover with Under-arm seam

Made from Shirt-waist Draft.

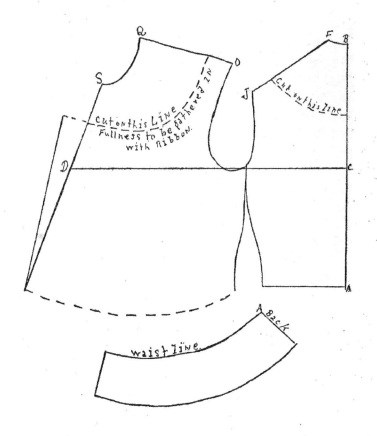

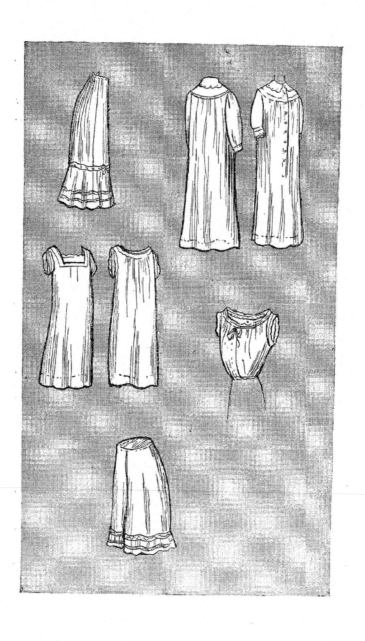

goods lengthwise. Sew the top of this piece to the bottom of the waist, having the seam on the wrong side   Before stitching, baste a straight band about ¾ of an inch wide so that it may be turned up over the seam. Stitch and turn the band up, having turned in the raw edge.   Work about 3 buttonholes down the right-hand hem and place buttons on the left hem   Have one at the top, one at the waist line, and one half way between.

LESSON XXXIII

SEAMLESS CORSET COVER MADE FROM THE SHIRT-WAIST DRAFT

1. Trace off on another piece of paper the back piece of the shirt-waist draft.

2 Measure towards the right from point V 1 inch. Connect this point with point T by a straight line.

3. Measure to the left of W 1 inch, and connect this point with T by a straight line

4. Lay these two lines on top of each other and trace off the waist.

5 Cut out in the neck as much as desired

6. Add to the front of the neck 3 inches   Point U.

7. Measure to the right of point X 3 inches.   Mark this V

8. Connect U and V with a straight line   This line is the front line of the corset cover

9. Cut all in one piece, laying the center back line on a fold of the goods lengthwise.

10. Gather the bottom, beginning about 2½ inches from the Under Arm for the back and 4 inches for the front (Y to V).

11. Finish the bottom with a circular frill, as given for the corset cover with Under Arm seam.

12. Gather the front at the neck, as given for the other corset cover.

Seamless Corset-cover

made from Shirt-waist Draft.

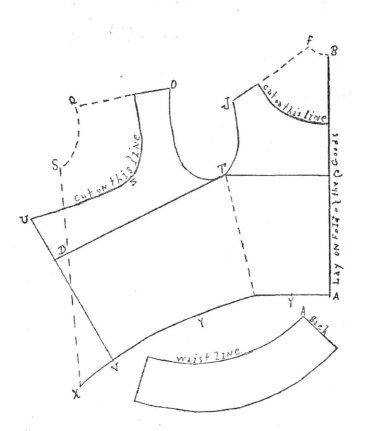

LESSON XXXIV

To take the measures —

Take waist measure as for dress.

Measure down the side of the leg from the waist line to just above the bend of the knee.

Measures used in draft given —

Waist measure	25	inches
Measure to knee	23	inches

Take a piece of paper having a square corner and one straight edge

1. Measure from the corner of the paper 2 inches.   Point A.

2 With A as a center and a radius of 10 inches, draw a circle, beginning at the edge of the paper.   Mark this circle B-C.

3. From B on this circle measure 1 inch.   Mark this point D.

4 From B, down the edge of the paper, measure 6 inches Mark this point E.

5. Connect D and E with a straight line.

6. Measure from point D on circle B-C 1 inch more than $\frac{1}{4}$ the Waist measure   Mark this point F.

7 From F on circle B-C measure 4 inches   Mark this point G.

8 Measure from point D, down the edge of the paper, the length of leg from waist to knee   Mark this point H

9. With the corner of the paper as a center and the distance from the corner to H as a radius, draw a circle from H.

10   On this circle from H measure 24 inches. Mark this point I.

11   Connect I and G with a straight line.

12   From G on line I-G measure 17¾ inches. Mark this point J.

13   Measure from I on circle H-I 1¾ inches. Mark this point K

14.   Connect points K and F with a straight line.

15   At J square a line with line G-I.

16   Place point J on the chart at J on the draft so that the curve just touches line F-K   Draw curve

This finishes the front portion of the drawers

To draft the back —

1   Measure from the corner of the paper 2 inches. Mark this point A

2.   With A as a center and a radius of 10 inches, draw a circle beginning at the edge of the paper   Mark this circle B-C.

3.   From B on circle B-C measure 1 inch. Mark this point D.

4.   From B, down the edge of the paper, measure 6 inches. Mark this point E.

5   Connect D and E with a straight line.

6.   Measure from D on circle B-C ¼ the Waist measure. Mark this point F.

7   Measure from F towards B on circle B-C, 1 inch. Mark this point G.

8   Measure from D, down the edge of the paper, the length of leg from waist to knee. Mark this point H.

9   Measure from point A, 2½ inches   Mark this point I

10   With I as a center and I-H as a radius, draw a circle from H

11   Measure from H, on this circle, 26 inches. Mark this point J

12   Connect J and G with a straight line.

13   Measure from G on line G-J, 20 inches. Mark this point K.

14. At point K square a line with line J-G.

15. Measure from K on this line 1½ inches.   Mark this point L.

16. Continue line L-K past K.

17. Measure on this line from K, 2 inches   Mark this point M.

18. Connect M and F with a straight line.

19. Place point J on the chart at L and hold chart so that the curve just touches line M-F   Draw curve

20 Connect J and L with a straight line

21. Place point D on the chart at point G and hold so that C on the chart just touches line F-M   Draw curve.

This finishes the back portion of the drawers

In cutting the pattern from the draft lay line E-H of the front on line E-H of the back as there should only be one piece for each leg of the drawers   There should be no seam at the side.

TO MAKE THE DIFFERENT SIZES

For every inch added to the waist, add 1 inch to curve H-I of the front and curve H-J of the back.   Also add ½ inch to G-J of the front and G-K of the back.

HOW TO CUT, MAKE AND FINISH THE CIRCULAR DRAWERS

Cut out two pieces of the material, one for each side. Sew line J-I to line L-J of each leg, making a fell seam. Sew line F-J of one front to line F-J of the other, beginning at point F and sewing for about 7 inches   This seam should be made a fell seam. (See Lesson I) Cut a bias band about 1 inch wide and sew to the rest of this line F-J, placing the bias band on the right side of the garment   Stitch in a seam about ¼ inch from the edge   Turn the band over on the wrong side of the garment, and after turning in the raw edge, stitch into place. Put a bias facing on lines G-L of both backs just as you have just been

Pattern of Womens Circular Drawers, cut from the Drafts.

Womens Circular Drawers.

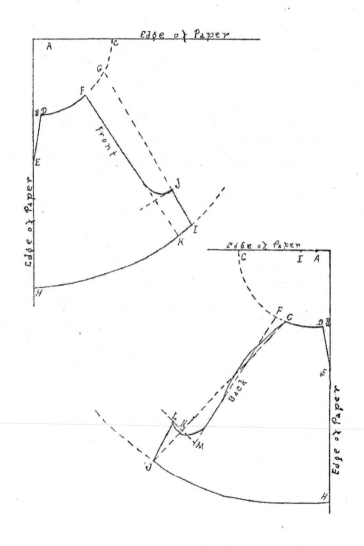

taught to do on the fronts   Sew line D-E to line D-E at each side, making a fell seam.   Finish about the top with a bias facing, put on just as you did the other facings.   The lower edge of this one will have to be stretched, as it is put on a circle.   This finishes the drawers except the bottoms of the legs   These may be finished just with a little lace edge, or they may have a ruffle 2½ or 3 inches wide   The draft was made full length, so it must be cut off as much at the bottom as the trimming is wide.   Sew one edge of the facing about the bottom at the same time you sew the ruffle, turn in the raw edge, and turn the facing up to form a narrow hem.   Three buttons and buttonholes should be placed down the back, beginning at G, about 2 inches apart. Rather large buttons are best.

LESSON XXXV

DRAFTING THE PRINCESS GOWN

THE waist part of the princess gown is drafted just like the tight waist with French forms

Measures used for draft given —

Waist measure	25 inches
Neck measure	13½ inches
Armhole measure	15 inches
Bust measure	39 inches
Back Width measure	13½ inches
Under Arm measure	7¾ inches
Front Length measure	15½ inches
Upper Front measure	10¾ inches
Back Length measure	16 inches

1. Draw line A-B length of Back measure.

2. Measure from A the Under Arm measure. Mark this point C.

3. B to D is ½ inch

4. At D square a line with A-D.

5. Measure from D on this line 1½ inches. Mark this point E.

6. Place point O on the chart at B and draw curve through E.

7. At C square a line with A-B

8. C to F is ½ of Bust measure

9 From C on line C-F measure ½ of back width   Mark this point G.

10. At G square a line with line C-F.

11 Measure on this line from point G 1-3 of Armhole measure. Mark this point H.

157

12 Place point D on the chart at point E, and draw curve through H. Extend curve ½ inch beyond H.

13 Extend line G-H above H 1¾ inches Mark this point I.

14 At I square a line with line G-I

15. On this line measure from I 2 inches. Mark this point J

16 From G on line C-F measure ¼ of Armhole measure. Mark this point K

17. Find a point half way between K and G. Mark this point L

18. At K square a line with C-F

19. Measure on this line 2½ inches from K Mark this point M.

20 Measure full length of curve E-H, and measure the same length from J on line I-J, extended Mark this point N.

21 Place point G on the chart at H and draw curve through L.

22 Place point O on the chart at M and draw curve through L

23. Place point F on the chart at M and draw a curve through J

24 Square a line with line C-F so that it will pass through N

25 Measure on this line from C-F the Upper Front measure, less what is used in the back neck. Mark this point O

26. Place point D on the chart at O and draw curve through J

27 From O measure on this line ¼ of Neck measure Mark this point P

28 At P square a line with line O-P.

29 Measure on this line from P 1-6 of the Neck measure and add ¼ inch Mark this point Q

30 Place point J on the chart at Q and draw curve through O

31 From Q draw line through F.

32. From Q on this line measure the Front length measure Mark this point R

33. At L square a line with line C-F.

34. Measure on this line from L the Under Arm measure. Mark this point S

35 Connect S and A with a straight line

36 From A on this line measure ¾ of an inch Mark this point T.

37. Connect T and B with a straight line.

38 Measure on the shoulder curve 2 inches from the Arm-hole. Mark this point U

39 Find a point half way between T and S Measure ½ inch to the left of this point Mark this point V

40. From V measure 1¼ inches to the right. Mark this point W.

41. Connect U and W with a straight line

42. Place point C on the chart at V and let point D touch line U-W Draw curve.

43. Measure to the right of S, 1 inch. Mark this point X.

44. Place point D on the chart at L and draw curve through X.

45. Measure to the left of S, 1½ inches Mark this point Y

46. Place point A on the chart at Y and draw curve through L.

47. Measure from T to W and from V to X This shows how much of the ½ Waist measure has been used in the back.

48 From point Y towards R measure what is left of the ½ Waist measure after taking out what is used in the back. Mark this point

49. Measure the distance from this point to point R.

This gives what must be taken out in the dart to bring the waist in to the desired measure. In this case it is 4½ inches.

50 Place point C on the chart at R and with curve C-F draw curve to S.

51. Measure from J on curve J-O, 2 inches. Mark this point Z.

52. Measure from R 2½ inches   Mark this point a.

53. Connect a and Z with a straight line

54 Measure from a on line a-Z 8 inches for a tall figure and 6 for a short figure. Mark this point c.

55. Measure to the right of a 4½ inches, or the amount to be taken out in the dart. Mark this point b.

56. Place point B on the chart at c and with curve A-B connect c with b.

57 Measure down from R 5 inches and from this point measure to the right ¼ inch more than from R to a. Mark this point e.

58. Draw a straight line from a through e and continue it the length of the front skirt measure. Point f

59 Continue line Q-F-R down the length of front skirt measure. Point d.

60. Connect d and f with a straight line

61 Square a line at b with line a-b and continue it down the length of front skirt measure.

62 Continue line L-S down below S 5 inches   Mark this point h

63. Measure 1 inch to the right of h   Mark this point i.

64 Place point D on the chart at Y and draw curve through i. Extend line down the length of side skirt measure. The slant of this line will depend on how full the skirts are being worn

65 Draw straight line from X through h   Continue down length of side skirt measure

66 Find a point half way between V and W and square a line with line V-W and draw 5 inches long. Mark this point j

67 Draw straight line from V through j and continue down length of back skirt measure.

68. From W draw straight line through j and continue down length of back skirt measure

Princess Gown.

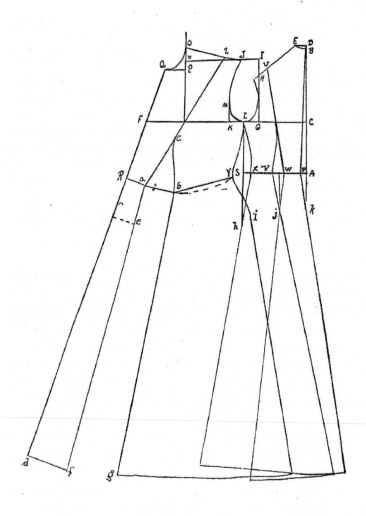

69. Continue line A-B 5 inches below A. Mark this point k.

70. From T draw straight line through k. Continue down length of back measure.

The slant of all the lines to 5 inches below the waist measure will depend on the hip measure   From this point down it depends entirely on the fullness of the skirts being worn. The back lines should always slant more than the front, to fit over the large part of the hips.

The draft given makes a medium width skirt.

LESSON XXXVI

DRAFTING THE SINGLE - BREASTED, TIGHT - FITTING, TAILORED
COAT

In drafting the coat some of the measures must be increased, as the coat is made to go on over the dress

We add 1 inch to Waist measure	26 inches
Neck measure same as for dress	13½ inches
Add 1 inch to Armhole measure .	16 inches
Add 1 inch to Bust measure	40 inches
Add ½ inch to Back Width measure	14 inches
Under Arm same as for dress	7¾ inches
Front Length same as for dress	15½ inches
Add ½ inch to Upper Front	11¼ inches
Back Length same as for dress .	16 inches

1. Draw A-B length of back.

2. Measure on line A-B from A the Under Arm measure. Mark this point C.

3. Continue line A-B above B ¾ of an inch. Mark this point D.

4 At D square a line with line A-B.

5. Measure from D on this line 1¾ inches   Mark this point E.

6. Place point O on the chart at B and draw curve through E.

7. At C square a line with line A-B

8. Measure from C on this line ½ the Bust measure   Mark this point F.

9. Measure from C on line C-F the Back Width measure. Mark point G.

10. At G square a line with line C-F.

11. Measure on this line 1-3 of the Armhole measure. Mark this point H.

12. Place point D on the chart at E and draw curve through H. Extend curve ½ inch beyond H.

13. Extend line G-H above H 1¾ inches. Mark this point I.

14. At I square a line with line G-I.

15. Measure from I on this line 2 inches. Mark this point J.

16. Measure to left of G on line C-F ¼ the Armhole measure. Mark this point K.

17 Find a point half way between G and K. Mark this point L.

18. At K square a line with C-F.

19. From K measure on this line 2¾ inches. Mark this point M.

20. Place point G on the chart at the end of curve E-H and draw curve through L

21. Place point O on the chart at M and draw curve through L.

22. Place point F on the chart at M and draw curve through J.

23. Extend line I-J.

24. Measure the full length of curve E-H and measure the same distance from J. Mark this point N

25. Square a line with line C-F so that it will pass through N.

26. Measure on this line from line C-F the Upper Front measure, less what is used in the back neck. Mark point O.

27. Place point D on the chart at O and draw curve through J.

28 Measure from O on line O-N ½ the Neck measure. Mark this point P.

29. At P square a line with line O-N

30. From P on this line, measure 1-3 the Neck measure plus ¼ inch. Mark this point Q.

31. Place point N on the chart at O and draw curve through Q.

32. Draw a straight line from Q through F.

33. Measure on this line from Q the Front Length measure. Mark this point R.

34. Find a point half way between K and L. Mark this point S.

35. At S square a line with line C-F.

36 Measure from S on this line the Under Arm measure. Mark this point T.

37. Connect T and A with a straight line.

38. Measure on this line from A, ½ of an inch. Mark this point U.

39. Connect U and B with a straight line.

40. Measure from U, 1¼ inches. Mark this point V.

41. Find a point half way between E and the other end of curve E-H. Mark this point W

42. Connect W and V with a straight line.

43. Measure from V, 1¼ inches. Mark this point X

44. Place point C on the chart at X and allow point D to touch line W-V. Draw curve.

45 Measure to the right of T, 1 inch. Mark this point Y.

46. Place point D on the chart at S and draw curve through Y.

47. Find a point half way between Y and X Mark this point Z.

48. Measure to the right of Z, ¼ of an inch Mark this point a.

49. Measure to the right of a, 1 inch Mark this point b

50. Place point C on the chart at b, and with curve C-F draw curve through G and continue to Armhole line

51. Place point C on the chart at a and allow D to touch curve G-b. Draw curve.

52. Measure to the left of T 1½ inches. Mark this point c.

53 Place point A on the chart at c and draw curve through S.

54. Place point C on the chart at R and with curve C-F draw curve through c.

55. From R measure to the right 3 inches. Mark this point d.

56. Measure from O on curve J-O the same distance as E to W. Mark point e

57. Connect e and d with a straight line.

58. Measure up from d on line d-e, 8 inches for slender form, and 6 for full form. Mark this point f.

59. Find on the tape-line, ½ of the Waist measure. Place this point at U and measure from U to V, then from X to b, then from a to Y. Place the point on the tape-line which falls at Y, at point c and with the rest of the Waist measure, measure towards R. Mark where the end of the tape-line falls.

60. From this point to R is the amount which must be taken out in the dart to bring the coat in to the desired measure. In this case it is 5 inches.

61 Measure from d on curve R-c the amount to be taken out in the dart Mark this point g.

62. Place point B on the chart at f and draw curve through g.

TO FORM SKIRT OF COAT

63. Continue line A-B below A 5 inches. Mark this point h

64. Connect U and h with a straight line. Continue line down as long as the coat is to be.

65. Find a point half way between V and X Mark this point i

66 At i square a line with line A-T

67. Measure from i on this line 5 inches. Mark this point j.

68 Connect j with V and with X by straight lines Continue lines down to bottom of coat.

69. Find a point half way between a and b. Mark this point k

70 At k square a line with line A-T.

71. Measure from k on this line 5 inches. Mark this point l.

72. Connect l with a and with b by a straight line. Continue line down the length of the coat.

73. Continue line S-T below T 5 inches Mark this point m.

74. Connect Y with m by a straight line and continue line down the length of coat

75. Measure to the right of m, 1 inch. Mark this point n.

76. Place point F on the chart at c and draw curve through n.

77. Square a line at g with the straight line from d to g. Draw line the length of the coat.

78. Measure down from R, 5 inches. Mark this point o.

79. Square a line with line Q-R at o

80. Measure from o on this line $\frac{1}{4}$ of an inch more than from R to d. Mark this point p.

81. Draw a straight line from d through p and continue down the length of the coat

This forms the skirt of the coat, making a coat of medium fullness The fullness must be governed by the coats being worn Draw the lines from the hips down, more or less slanting as desired

The coat, as it is, just comes together in front. We must add something for lap for buttons and buttonholes

82. At F square a line with line Q-R and measure from F 2 inches. Mark this point q.

83. At R square a line with line Q-R and measure from R, 2 inches. Mark this point r.

84. Draw a line through q and r the full length of coat.

85. Continue line P-Q out to q-r. Mark this point s

86. Measure down from s, $\frac{1}{4}$ of an inch Mark this point t.

87. Connect Q and t with a straight line.

88 Measure from t on line t-q, 8 inches, or any desired distance Mark this point u.

89. Continue line J-N until it touches the neck curve. Mark this point v.

Single Breasted Tight-fitting Coat.

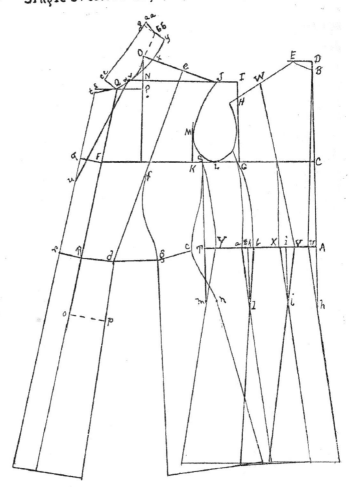

90. Measure down from v on the neck curve, ½ inch. Mark this point w

91 Connect w and u with a straight line. This forms the LAPEL.

TO DRAFT THE COLLAR

92 Measure from O on the shoulder curve, ½ inch. Mark this point x.

93 Place point D on the chart at v and draw curve through x

94. Extend this curve beyond x as much as the back neck measures. Mark this point y.

95. Connect y and x with a straight line.

96. Square a line with this line at y.

97. Measure on this line from y, 2½ inches. Mark this point z.

98 Measure to the right from z, ¼ inch. Mark this point aa.

99 Measure from y on line y-z 1 inch Mark this point bb.

100. Connect aa and bb with a straight line

101. Square a line with line w-u, so that it will run through point Q.

102. Measure from Q, 1¼ inches Mark this point cc

103. Place point B on the chart at aa and draw curve through cc.

104. Place point C on the chart at v and draw curve through bb.

LESSON XXXVII

LOOSE-FITTING UNLINED COAT

MEASURES used for this draft —

Neck measure	13 inches
Armhole measure ...	17 inches
Bust measure	40 inches
Back Width measure .	14 inches
Under Arm measure	7¾ inches
Front Length measure	15½ inches
Upper Front measure	11¼ inches
Back Length measure	16 inches
Length from back of neck straight down back to bottom of coat	58½ inches
Length from front of neck, straight down front to bottom of coat	55½ inches

1. Draw line A-B length of back to waist line.

2. From A measure on line A-B Under Arm measure. Mark this point C

3. From B measure up ½ inch   Mark this point D

4 At D square a line with A-D

5. From D on this line measure 1¾ inches. Mark this point E.

6. Place point O on the chart at B, and draw curve through E.

7. At C square a line with line A-B

8. From C measure on this line ½ of Bust measure   Mark this point F.

9. From C on line C-F measure ½ of Back Width measure. Mark this point G.

10. At G square a line with line C-F.

11. Measure from G on this line $\frac{1}{3}$ of Armhole measure. Mark this point H

12. Continue the line above H 1¾ inches. Mark this point I.

13. Place point D on the chart at E and draw curve through H. Extend curve ½ inch beyond H.

14. At I square a line with line G-I

15 From I on this line measure 2 inches   Mark this point J.

16 From G on line C-F measure ¼ of Armhole measure. Mark this point K.

17 Find a point half way between G and K   Mark this point L.

18. At K square a line with line C-F. Mark this point M

19. Place point G on the chart at end of curve E-H and draw curve through L

20. Place point O on the chart at M and draw curve through L.

21 Place point F on the chart at M and draw curve through J.

22. Continue line I-J to the left.

23. From J on this line measure the same distance as the full length of curve E-H   Mark this point N

24. Square a line with line C-F so that it will pass through N.

25. From line C-F, measure on this line the Upper Front measure less what is used in the back neck   Mark this point O.

26. Place point D on the chart at O and draw curve through J.

27. From O measure down ½ of Neck measure. Mark this point P

28 At P square a line with line O-P.

29 Measure from P on this line 1-3 of Neck measure, plus ¼ inch. Mark this point Q.

30. Place point J on the chart at Q and draw curve through O.

Loose Fitting Unlined Coat.

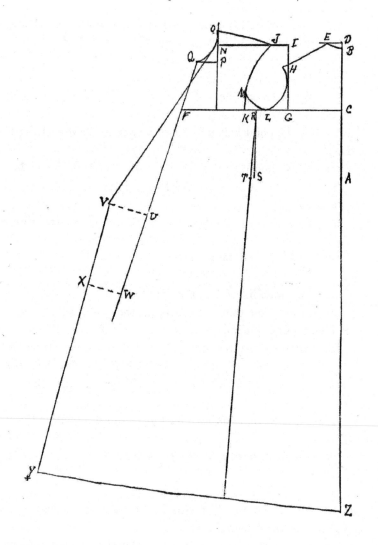

31   Draw straight line from Q through F.

32.   Find a point half way between K and L   Mark this point R.

33.   At R square a line with line C-F.

34   Measure on this line from R, the Under Arm measure. Mark this point S

35   Measure to the left of S, ¾ of an inch.   Mark this point T.

36.   Draw a straight line from R through T and continue it down the length of the coat

37.   Measure down from Q on line Q-F the length you wish your coat to open in the neck.   Mark this point U.

38   At U square a line with line Q-U.

39.   Measure on this line from U 4 inches, for the lap of the coat in front (double-breasted).   Mark this point V.

40.   Connect point V and a point on the neck curve opposite point N with a straight line.

41   Measure down from U any convenient distance.   Mark point W

42.   At W square a line with line Q-W.

43.   Measure from W on this line ½ inch less than from U to V   Mark this point X.

44   Draw a straight line from V through X and continue down the length of coat.   Point Y.

45.   Continue line A-B down the length of coat.

The line R-T forms the under arm line for both front and back.

If more fullness is desired, measure 1 inch from S to T, instead of ¾ of an inch, and measure ¾ of an inch to the right of S. Draw lines from R through these points   These coats are usually made up without a collar or with a large sailor collar.   The sleeves may be made a medium sized flowing sleeve or the regulation coat sleeve.

LESSON XXXVIII

Measures used for draft given —

Waist measure	26 inches
Neck measure	13½ inches
Armhole measure	16 inches
Bust measure	20 inches
Back Width measure	14 inches
Under Arm measure	7¼ inches
Front Length measure	15½ inches
Upper Front measure	11¼ inches
Back Length measure	16 inches

1. Draw A-B length of back.

2. From A measure the Under Arm measure. Mark this point C

3. Measure above B, ½ inch   Mark this point D.

4. At D square a line with line A-D.

5. From D on this line measure 1¾ inches. Mark this point E.

6. At C square a line with line A-B.

7. Measure from C on this line the Bust measure. Mark this point F

8 From C on line C-F measure the Back Width. Mark this point G.

9 At G square a line with line C-F.

10. Measure from G on this line 1-3 of Armhole measure. Mark this point H.

11. Place point D on the chart at E and draw curve through H. Extend curve ½ inch beyond H.

175

12. Extend line G-H above H 1½ inches. Mark this point I.

13. At I square a line with line G-I.

14. From I on this line measure 2 inches. Mark this point J

15 Measure from G on line C-F ¼ the Armhole measure. Mark this point K.

16 Find a point half way between K and G. Mark this point L

17 At K square a line with line C-F.

18 Measure from K on this line 2½ inches.   Mark this point M

19 Place point G on the chart at the end of curve E-H and draw curve through L.

20. Place point O on the chart at M and draw curve through L.

21. Place point F on the chart at M and draw curve through J

22 Measure curve E-H and measure the same distance from J. Mark this point N.

23 Square a line with line C-F so that it will pass through point N

24. Measure from line C-F on this line the Upper Front measure, less what is used in the back neck   Mark this point O

25. Measure down from O, ¼ the Neck measure. Mark this point P

26 At P square a line with line O-P.

27. Measure from P on this line 1-6 of Neck measure. Mark this point Q

28. Place point N on the chart at O and draw curve through Q

29 Draw a line from Q through F

30. Measure from Q on this line the Front Length. Mark this point R.

31. At L, square a line with line F-C.

32 Measure from L on this line the Under Arm measure. Mark this point S.

33. Connect S and A with a straight line.

34. Measure from A, 1-3 the distance from A to S. Mark this point T.

35 Measure ½ inch to the left of T   Mark this point U

36. Find a point half way between E and the end of curve E-H   Mark this point V.

37. Connect U and V with a straight line.

38. Measure to the left of U, ½ inch. Mark this point W.

39. Place point C on the chart at W and allow curve to touch line U-V. Draw curve.

40. Measure to the right of S, ½ inch   Mark this point X.

41. Place point C on the chart at L and draw curve through X.

42 Measure to the left of S, 1 inch   Mark this point Y

43. Place point B on chart at L and draw curve through Y

44. Measure from R 1-3 the distance from R to Y. Mark this point Z.

45 Measure from E to V, and measure this same distance from O. Mark this point a.

46. Connect a and Z with a straight line.

47. Find out how much should be taken out on the dart to bring the coat in tight to the waist and take out about 2-3 of this amount   Mark this point b

48. Draw a straight line from b to the point where line C-F crosses line a-Z.

49 Continue line Q-R below A 6 inches.

50. Measure from c square over ½ inch more than from R to z   Mark this point d.

51. Connect d and Z by a straight line.

52. Connect Z and b with a straight line and square a line with this line at b

53. Measure down 6 inches. Mark this point e.

54. Continue line A-B below a 6 inches   Mark this point f.

55. Find a point half way between W and U. Mark this point g

56 Square a line at g with line A-S.

57 Measure down from g 6 inches. Mark this point h.

58 Connect h with U and W by straight lines

59 Continue line L-S down 6 inches. Mark this point i

60 Connect i with X and Y by straight lines

61 Square a line with line Q-R at F

62 Measure from F on this line 4 inches. Mark this point j

63. Square a line with line Q-R at a point $1\frac{1}{4}$ inches below Q on line Q-R.

64 Measure from Q on this line 4 inches. Mark this point k

65. Connect k and j with a straight line

66. Measure from k on line k-j 9 inches, or as much as you wish the coat to open in front. Mark this point l.

67. Measure down $\frac{1}{2}$ inch from where line J-N meets the neck curve Mark this point m.

68. Connect m and l with a straight line This forms the LAPEL

In making the coat lap the fronts so that line Q-R of one side falls on line Q-R of the other.

TO DRAFT THE COLLAR

69 Measure from O on the shoulder curve $\frac{3}{4}$ of an inch. Mark this point n.

70 Place point D on the chart at m and draw curve through n Extend curve as much beyond n as the back of the neck measures. Mark this point o

71. Square a line at o with a straight line from n to o.

72 Measure from o on this line $1\frac{1}{2}$ inches.   Mark this point p.

73 Continue the line up from p $1\frac{1}{2}$ inches. Mark this point q

Slightly Fitted Coat.

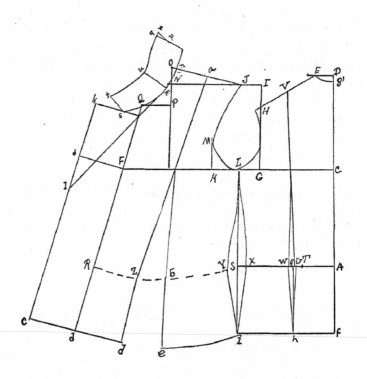

74. Measure to the right of q ¼ inch. Mark this point r.

75. Measure from k 2¾ inches   Mark this point s.

76. Place point D on the chart at m and draw curve through s.

77. Place point D on the chart at p and draw curve through m (break of collar)

78. Square a line with line m-l so that it passes through s

79. Measure from s on this line 2 inches. Mark this point t.

80. Square a line with line m-l at m.

81. Measure from m on this line 2¼ inches. Mark this point u.

82. Place point B on chart at r and draw curve through u.

83. Place point F on chart at t and draw curve through u.

LESSON XXXIX

WE have taught you how to draft the coat. This is a comparatively easy thing, but to make the coat is one of the most difficult things the dressmaker is called upon to do. However, if you follow our directions carefully you will have little trouble.

After having made your draft, make a pattern, just as you were taught to do in making the gowns. Lay the pattern on the goods, having the wrong side of the goods up. If the goods has a nap, this should run down. BE SURE TO HAVE THE WAIST LINE OF THE PATTERN ON THE STRAIGHT OF THE GOODS CROSSWISE. Mark carefully all seams and the waist line with tailor's chalk, also mark where the pockets are to be. Mark the line which is the turn of the lapel, where the bottom of the coat should be, and for the buttons and buttonholes After these lines have all been marked with the chalk, trace on all of them with a running stitch, using a thread of a contrasting color from the goods. Be very careful to keep exactly on the line. We are now ready to shrink and stretch the different parts, to give it the desired curves. It is the curve which gives the garment style. The directions we give will be for the fitted coat. The loose coat and the semi-fitted will not need it

A large tailor's iron must always be used in making the tailored garment The main reason why a dressmaker's coat seldom has the style of the tailored garment is because it is nearly always pressed with a common flat-iron The iron which is used by the tailor is never lighter than 15 pounds, while the ordinary flat-iron only weighs about 3 or 4 pounds Heat the iron as hot as it can be used without scorching Never use it on the bare goods and never on the right side of the goods. Use a clean sponge to dampen the goods and a piece of clean muslin without starch to place between the goods and the iron Have a flat ironing-board, not too heavily padded It must be hard enough to give the goods a very dead press We are ready to proceed with the shrinking and stretching With the wet sponge dampen a line on each piece, represented in the drawing by letters A, B, C, D. While they are still wet, place the iron on them Be very careful to have the goods perfectly smooth under the iron If any little creases are pressed in it is very difficult to get them out. This is all there is to the shrinking process, but as simple as it may seem, it is really difficult and needs considerable practice. Now we will begin to stretch the seams, to give the desired curve. For this you must study the form for which the garment is being made For a very full form you will need to stretch the seams quite a bit, while for a very slender person they will only be stretched a very little

Take the front piece first. Dampen with the sponge the under arm seam at the waist line and a little above and below While it is wet, place it on the board, and as it is pressed stretch it as desired. Now dampen the place which comes at the highest part of the bust (indicated by a cross on the drawing) Stretch this by moving the iron about in a small circle Take great care not to stretch it too much, as the curve of the seam will give nearly all that is needed Take the under arm piece and stretch each edge at the waist line as you did the front, also stretch the waist line at point a. The back pieces will not need to be stretched, unless for a very full form, as the back is straighter than the front and does not need so much curve. Be careful to stretch each seam the same amount

We are ready now to sew up the seams Sew the two front pieces together first. Before beginning to baste, pin the seams at the waist line, then at the shoulder, and in between these points every few inches, as in basting one side will stretch more than the other Continue the pinning down to the bottom of the coat Now baste the seam with a running stitch, taking rather small, even stitches. Next pin and baste the two back form pieces together in the same way. The seams next to the middle back seam are usually left open for about 4 or 5 inches from the bottom, if it is a short jacket. If a long coat, then the back seam is left open instead of the side ones, from the waist line to the bottom of the coat. When these seams are left open a piece must be cut on one side of the seam to run under the opening Baste the front to the under arm piece, and last of all the back parts to the under arm piece, in each case beginning at the under arm piece and working both ways Stitch the seams, dampen and press open. If the goods has a nap the seams should be scraped before pressing Scrape against the nap with a dull knife or shears This gives a flatter appearance to the seam when pressed.

If pockets are put in the coat they must be located with great care. No matter how well the coat is made, if the pockets are badly located the coat will look home-made. Until you learn by practice just where the pocket should be, you will have to locate them by placing the garment on the patron and placing them where they look the best You will soon learn to tell very nearly where they should be. To put in the pocket — Place a piece of linen canvas back of the marking for the pocket. Make a smooth straight cut on the line of basting Cut two pieces of the goods thus, ⌣ about 1 inch longer than the cut, these two pieces are the pocket Lay one of the pieces on the right side of the coat, so that the top edge comes just even with the lower side of the cut Have the right side of the goods together Stitch across on the machine, making a very small seam Push this piece of the pocket through the opening, and turn down so that a little of the pocket shows from the right side, like a small cord Stitch across on the right side near the first stitching Now make a flap for the pocket. Cut a piece of the goods about 2¾ inches wide and ½ inch longer than the opening of the pocket Turn the ends in a little more than ¼ inch, and one long side the same amount Dampen and press a dead press Fit a piece of the material to be used for the coat lining to this piece of goods,

turning in all the edges, except the one unfinished side. Do not
have the lining come quite to the edge. Press again without
dampening, and stitch about the three sides so that the stitching will catch the lining. This finishes the flap for the pocket.
The flap when it is finished should be just the size of the opening.
Place the flap with its right side against the right side of the
coat, above the opening, so that its unfinished edge is just even
with the upper side of the opening Stitch across, making a very
small seam. Turn the flap down over the opening, and turn the
seam up and baste on the outside near the first stitching. Put
the right side of this piece against the right side of the coat Now
lay the other piece of the pocket on the wrong side of the coat
so that the straight side is just above this last basting; stitch
on this basting, being careful to catch the pocket. Turn the coat
over The two pieces which form the pocket will lie one on top
of the other. Stitch them together in a flat seam. Stitch twice
so they will not rip The front edge of the flap should always
follow the front edge of the coat. This is the most common way
of finishing the pocket. There are many fancy ways to be found
on the ready-made garments. Keep your eyes open and you
will learn many of them

Now we must put the canvas in the coat If the coat is made
of rather light goods, the entire coat should be lined with a light
weight cotton canvas, which may be bought at any dry goods
store. If the goods is firm and heavy this interlining need not
be used The canvas must be tailor's canvas, and not the kind
used by dressmakers for many purposes. Spread the canvas
flat on the ironing-board Wet a large piece of muslin very wet
and spread over it. Iron with a very hot iron until the cloth
is dry Turn the canvas over and place the wet cloth on this
side and press dry. Remove the cloth and press the canvas
until thoroughly dry Spread the canvas on the cutting-table
and put the pattern on it. Trace the shape shown in the drawing,
remove the pattern and cut out In cutting this piece the lengthwise threads of the canvas should follow the edge of the coat.

Slash the edge of the canvas in about 1½ inches where it comes over the most prominent part of the bust, half way between the neck and armhole at the shoulder seam, and about 2 inches from the shoulder seam in the neck. Stretch these slashes open and baste pieces of canvas back of them so that they cannot come together again. Dampen the canvas where the prominent part of the bust comes and stretch to form the proper shape. Two of these pieces should be prepared, one for each side of the coat. Baste them into place, having the edge of the canvas come even with the coat. Cut the canvas back about ¼ of an inch from the edge of the cloth. Now we must pad the lapels with the padding stitch. These stitches should be short and near together. Begin at the line for the turn of the lapel. Take the stitches through the canvas and into the goods, but not through it so that it shows on the right side. Completely fill the lapel with stitches, done in rows following the line of turning. As the work is done cause the lapel to have a slight curl. This will cause it to turn more gracefully and give style to the garment. Provide yourself with some stay tape. Fasten this about the edge, putting it on rather tightly. Do not allow the stitches where it is fastened to show on the right side. Dampen and press dry. Now sew up the shoulder seams, without catching in the canvas. Press with a dead press and allow the canvas to lie flat over the seam. Cut two pieces of the goods the same shape as the canvas, for a facing of the coat. Baste the edges of the facing to the edges of the coat, having the right side of the facing against the right side of the coat. Stitch the edges as near the stay tape as possible. Turn the facing over on the wrong side of the coat and baste the edges together, making a straight, even edge. Be sure that the corner of the lapel is pulled out so that it makes a good shaped corner. Roll the lapel over as it should roll when finished and baste the facing along the line of turning. Baste the back edge of the facing to the coat. Cut a piece of the light canvas which was used for the interlining, on the bias, about 1½ inches wide. Fold this through the center lengthwise and baste the turned edge along the thread where the coat is to turn up about the bottom. Use short stitches in basting this so that it will stay exactly on the thread. Turn the goods up on this canvas, being sure to turn on the exact line for the bottom We are ready to put on the collar. Trace off the collar from the draft on another piece of paper and cut out, allowing ¼ inch seams everywhere Have the right sides of the goods together and cut two pieces together. Before raising the pattern from the goods, mark the back seam Stitch this, open and press Cut two pieces of canvas on the bias by the same pattern. Stitch the back seam and press open. Lay the back seam of the canvas on the back seam of the goods, having the canvas on the wrong side of the goods. Baste the canvas and the cloth together thoroughly. Cut the canvas away from the outside edge and at the ends about ¼ inch Fasten the canvas to the goods with a padding stitch, stretching the goods a little tighter than the canvas, so that the collar will roll as it should when on the coat. The padding should be done from the canvas side After this is thoroughly done, stitch the collar with straight rows of stitching until the point is reached where the collar turns From this point to the outer edge stitch with a row of zig-zag stitching extending the full length of the collar Thus —

Cut another piece from the goods by the same pattern but having no seam in the back Lay the back edge of the pattern on fold of the goods length-wise Allow about ¼ inch on the neck edge and allow seams as you did on the other pieces Baste this piece to the collar you have prepared, having the right sides of the goods together Stitch on the machine along the two ends and the outside edge, near the edge of the canvas Turn the collar so that both sides are of the goods and the canvas is between Baste along the edge, making a smooth even, edge Pin the back seam of the collar, leaving the outside piece of the goods loose, to the back seam of the coat Have the under side of the collar against the right side of the coat Pin the neck edge of the collar each way from the seam to the neck of the coat so that the ends of the collar come at point Q on the draft, or 1¾ inches from the point of the lapels. Baste this seam firmly and stitch on the machine. Dampen and press open, taking great care not to spoil the curve. Bring the right side of the collar over smoothly and baste along the line of turning. Bring it on over to the neck seam, and baste. You will find that there is a little seam where the facing and the collar meet at each end, which is not stitched. Bring the seam together neatly so that it will follow the seam underneath it and blind stitch with very small stitches Stitch all about the edge of the coat about ¼ inch from the edge. Be very careful when you stitch about the lapels and collar to turn good square corners

We are ready now to line the coat Cut the back pieces of the lining ¾ of an inch larger than the pattern at the back seam. Cut the side pieces the same as the pattern Cut the front side pieces the same as the pattern, but when you cut the front pieces, lay a plait in the goods about the center of the shoulder seam and about 1 inch deep at the shoulder seam, allowing it to taper out to nothing as it comes down to the bust. Allow enough to turn in where the lining comes on to the front facing Baste up all but the shoulder and under arm seams   Stitch and press. Baste the back seam to the back seam of the coat Baste all about the armholes and at the shoulder and under arm seams. Turn in the neck and baste down Baste the fronts in about the armholes. Turn in the shoulder seams and baste down flat to the back shoulder seams. Turn in the under arm seam and baste flat to the back portion Turn in down the front and baste to the back edge of the facing. Turn up all about the bottom, keeping the lining away from the edge of the coat about 1-8 of an inch. Now hem the shoulder seams, the under arm seams, down the front, about the bottom and about the neck. The coat is all finished now but the sleeves

Cut the pattern and the sleeves from the goods just as you did for the dress sleeve. Baste up and try on. Get the exact length

Coat Showing where stretching
and shrinking is done, also piece
of canvas in front

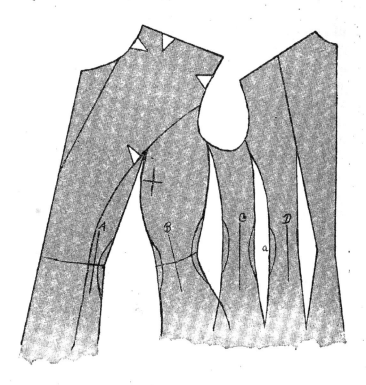

and run a thread marking where the sleeve is to turn. Stitch
up the inside seam and press open. Open the other seam and
spread the sleeves out on the table. Cut a piece of the tailor's
canvas 3½ inches wide and cover one edge with a piece of
cotton lining material cut on the bias.   Baste the piece of canvas to the sleeve so that the covered edge just follows the line
where the sleeve is to turn up   Baste the canvas to the sleeve
thoroughly and stitch up the outside seam of the sleeve. Press
open   Turn up the sleeve at the hand. Cut a lining by the same
pattern, stitch up and press. Place inside of the sleeve and the
seams together. Turn the lining up at the hand and hem to the
sleeve about 1 inch from the edge of the sleeve. Sew the sleeves
to the coat without catching the lining   Stitch in and bring the
lining up over the seam. Turn in and hem down.

LESSON XL

THE measures used are of a child 3 years of age.

Bust measure	24	inches
Neck measure	9½	inches
Waist measure	23	inches
Armhole measure	13	inches
Front Length measure	10	inches
Back Length measure	9	inches
Under Arm measure	4½	inches
Upper Front measure	8½	inches
Back Width measure	8	inches

1. Draw line A-B length of back.

2. Measure from A on line A-B the Under Arm measure. Mark this point C.

3. Continue line A-B above B ¼ inch. Mark this point D

4. At D square a line with line A-B.

5. From D measure on this line 1¼ inches. Mark this point E.

6. At C square a line with line A-B.

7. Measure from C on this line ½ of Bust measure   Mark this point F.

8. From C on line C-F measure ½ the Back Width measure. Mark this point G.

9. At G square a line.

10. Measure on this line from G 1-3 of Armhole measure. Mark this point H

11. Place point D on the chart at E and draw a curve through H. Extend curve ½ inch beyond H.

12. Continue line G-H above H 1½ inches. Mark this point I.

13 At I square a line with line G-I.

14. From I measure on this line 2 inches. Mark this point J.

15. From G on line C-F measure to the left ¼ of Armhole measure   Mark this point K.

16 Find a point half way between K and G. Mark this point L

17. At K square a line with line C-F.

18. Measure from K on this line 2 inches. Mark this point M

19. Place point G on the chart at the end of curve E-H and draw line touching line G-H.

20 Place point K on the chart at this point and draw curve through L

21. Place point K on the chart at M and draw curve through L.

22 Place point F on the chart at M and draw curve through J.

23. Measure the full length of curve E-H and measure the same distance from J on line I-J continued. Mark this point N.

24. Square a line with line C-F so that it will pass through N

25 Measure from line C-F on this line the Upper Front measure, less what is used in the back neck   Mark this point O

26 Place point D on the chart at O and draw curve through J

27. Measure down from O on line O-N ¼ of Neck measure. Mark this point P.

28. At P square a line with line O-N.

29. Measure from P on this line 1-6 of Neck measure and add ¼ inch. Mark this point Q

30 Place point J on the chart at Q and draw curve through O.

31. Draw a line from Q through F

32. Measure from Q on this line the Front Length measure. Mark this point R.

Childs' Draft.

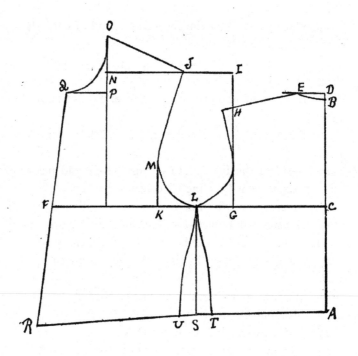

33. At L square a line with line C-F.

34. Measure from L on this line the Under Arm me Mark this point S.

35. Connect A and S with a straight line.

36. Connect S and R with a straight line.

37. Find out how much too large the Waist measure i this case it is 1¾ inches.

38. Measure half this distance to left of S and half to of S. Mark these points T and U.

39. Place point B on the chart at L and draw curve th T.

40. Place point B on the chart at L and draw curve th U.

In cutting out allow all seams.

LESSON XLI

CHILD'S SLEEVE DRAFT

MEASURES used for draft given —

Arm Length measure	8	inches
Arm Length to elbow	4	inches
Armhole measure	13	inches
Hand measure	6	inches

1. Draw A-B length of Arm.
2. From A measure length of Arm to bend of Elbow. Point C.
3. At A square a line with line A-B.
4. At B square a line with line A-B.
5. At C square a line with line A-B.
6. Measure from B on line, ½ inch. Mark this point D.
7. Measure from C, ¼ inch. Mark this point E.
8. Measure to the left of A, ½ inch. Mark this point F.
9. Place point D on the chart at E and draw curve to F.
10. Connect E and D with a straight line
11. Measure to the right of D, 1 inch   Mark this point G.
12. Measure to the right of G, 2 inches more than the Hand measure. Mark this point H.
13. Measure to the right of H, 1 inch. Mark this point I.
14. Extend line A-B above A, 1½ inches. Mark this point J.
15. Measure to the right of J, ½ inch. Mark this point K.
16. Measure from A, the Armhole measure. Mark this point L.
17. Measure to the left of L, 4 inches. Mark this point M.
18. Measure to the left of L, 1½ inches. Mark this point N.

Childs' Sleeve.

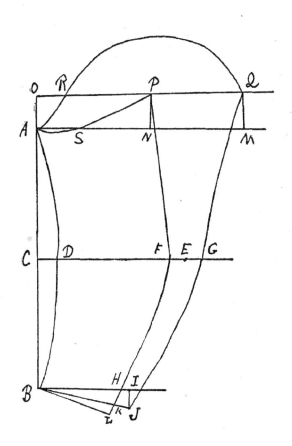

19. At M square a line with line A-L and extend line J-K to meet it. Point O.

20. At K square a line with line O-K and mark where it touches line A-L, P.

21. Place point D on the chart at L and draw curve to I.

22. Place point J on the chart at F and draw curve through K.

23. Place point F on the chart at O and draw curve to N.

24. Place point F on the chart at N and continue curve to L.

25. Find a point half way between P and M. Mark this point Q

26. With Q as a center and a radius Q-K, draw curve from K to O.

27. Find a point half way between D and I Mark this point R.

28. Square a line at R with line D-I and measure on this line from R, ½ inch. Mark this point S.

29. Place point D on the chart at S, and draw curves through D and I.

30. Gather the sleeve from 1 inch from D to 1 inch from I. Also from K to O.

LESSON XLII

CHILD'S COAT SLEEVE

MEASURES used for draft given —

Arm Length measure .	8	inches
Arm Length to elbow .	4	inches
Armhole measure .	13	inches
Hand measure	6	inches
Elbow measure .	8	inches

1. Draw A-B length of Arm.

2. Measure from A on line A-B length of Arm to bend of Elbow. Mark this point C.

3. Square a line with line A-B, at C.

4. Measure from C on this line ½ inch. Mark this point D.

5. Place point D on the chart at D and draw curves to A and B.

6. Square a line at B with line A-B.

7. Measure from B on this line ½ the Hand measure. Mark this point H.

8. Measure to the right of H ¼ inch. Mark this point I.

9. At I square a line with line B-I.

10. Measure from I on this line ½ inch. Mark this point J.

11. Connect J and B with a straight line.

12 Measure from J on this line ½ inch. Mark this point K.

13. Measure from D ½ of Elbow measure. Mark this point E.

14. Measure to the left and right of E ½ inch. Mark these points F and G

15 Place point F on the chart at F and draw curve through K.

Childs' Sleeve.

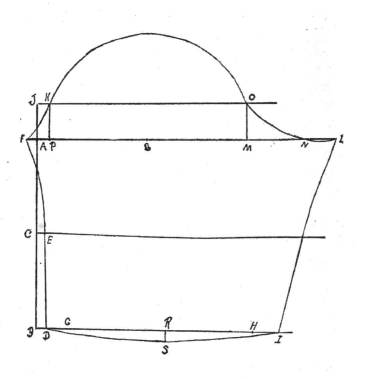

16. Place point F on the chart at G and draw curve through J.

17. Measure line G-J and add enough to line F-K to make it the same length. Mark this point L.

18. Connect L and B with a straight line.

19. At A square a line with line A-B.

20. Measure from A on this line ½ of Armhole measure. Mark this point M.

21. Measure to the left of M 3 inches. Mark this point N.

22. Continue line A-B above A, 1 inch. Mark this point O.

23. At O square a line with line B-O.

24. At N square a line with line A-M and mark point P, where it meets line from O

25. Square a line at M with line A-M and mark point Q, where it meets line from O.

26. Connect P and F with a straight line.

27. Place point D on the chart at G and draw curve to Q

28. Measure from O on line O-Q ½ inch. Mark this point R

29 Place point F on the chart at. R and draw curve to A.

30 Place point F on the chart at P and draw curve to S, which is 1 inch to the right of A. Continue curve to A.

31. Use N as a center and N-R as a radius and draw curve R-Q

In cutting pattern allow all seams.

LESSON XLIII

CHILD'S ROMPERS

THE rompers given are for a child of 3 years.

Use the same draft as for the child's waist.

1. Add 1 inch down the back line, S-T-U.

2. Add 2 inches to the bottom of the back waist portion, line W-V.

3. Add 1 inch to the front line X-Y-Z.

4. Leave out lines L-U and L-T of the waist draft.

5. For the back neck, measure from S, 2 inches.

6. To draft the trousers part of the rompers — Continue line L-S down below S, 5 inches.

7. Measure to the right of the end of this line $\frac{1}{2}$ inch. Mark this point a.

8. Connect a-S with a straight line.

9. Continue line X-Y-Z below Z, $12\frac{1}{2}$ inches. Mark this point b.

10. At b square a line with line Z-b and draw $22\frac{1}{2}$ inches long. Mark this point c.

11. Measure from b on line b-Z, 3 inches. Mark this point d.

12. Measure from b on line b-c, 3 inches. Mark this point e.

13. Place point J on the chart at e and draw curve through d.

14. At c square a line with line c-e.

15. Measure from c on this line, 1 inch. Mark this point f.

16. Draw a line from e through f and continue 5 inches beyond f. Mark this point g.

17. Measure from U on line U-T $1\frac{1}{2}$ inches. Mark this point h.

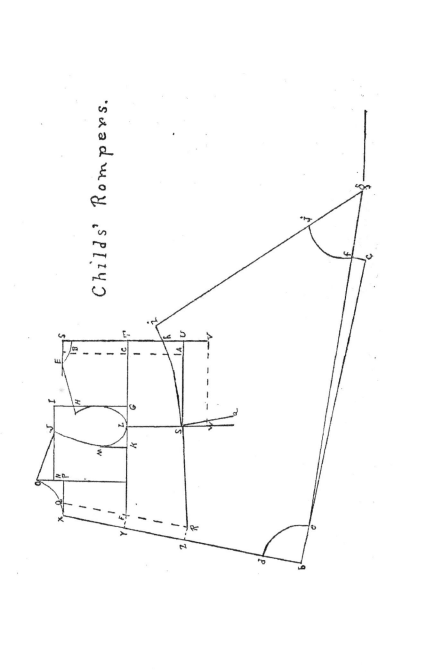

Child's' Rompers.

18. Place point D on the chart at S and draw curve through h

19. Continue curve 1 inch beyond i.

20. Connect g and i with a straight line.

21. Measure from g on line g-i 5 inches. Mark this point j.

22. Place point J on the chart at f and draw curve through j.

In cutting pattern allow all seams.

LESSON XLIV

HOW TO CUT AND FINISH THE ROMPERS

TRACE off on another piece of paper the front portion, allowing seams everywhere except down the front line X-Y-Z-d

Trace off the back, allowing seams everywhere except down the back line S-U-V, where $1\frac{1}{4}$ inches should be allowed

Cut on line S-a. This is the pattern for the ROMPERS

The amount of goods required for the Rompers — 27 inches wide, 2 1-8 yards; 36 inches wide, $1\frac{1}{2}$ yards, 44 inches wide, $1\frac{1}{4}$ yards.

To cut from the goods — Lay line X-Y-Z on a fold of the goods lengthwise and cut the front portion. Trace all seams before you raise the pattern from the goods. Lay the back on the double goods, having line W-V on the straight of the goods cross-wise.

Sew line d-e to line f-j.

Sew the shoulder seam of each back to the shoulder seam of each front.

Sew line L-S of each back to line L-S of the fronts.

Face each side, line S-a, with a continuous facing Turn the facing on the back under for a hem and leave the front projecting for an under lap

Sew line i-j of one side to i-j of the other

Gather line i-s of each side so that it fits on to line S-U of the back, and face it with a straight facing about $1\frac{1}{4}$ inches wide

Turn in the edges down the back 1 inch after having turned in the raw edge and stitch.

Finish the neck square or round, with either a bias band of the goods put on the right side or with embroidery insertion.

Sew buttons and work buttonholes down the back

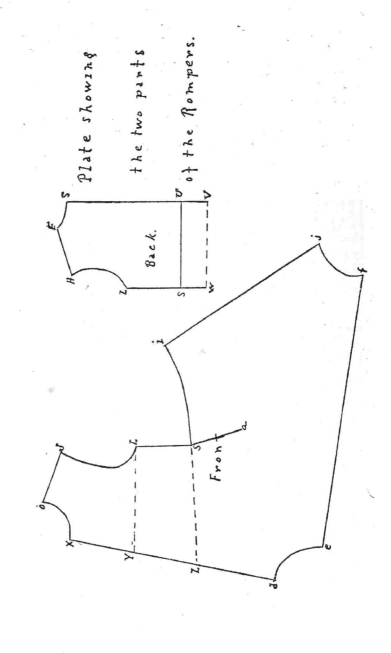

Plate showing
the two parts
of the Rompers.

Back.

Front

Work buttonholes along line S-i and place buttons along S-U.

Put a half-inch hem in the bottom of each leg and run elastic in the hems, just the size of the child's leg, but not tight.

For the sleeve use the Child's Full Sleeve Draft. Finish at the hand with a straight band or insertion .

Make a belt 1½ inches wide and fasten along the top of the back of the trousers part and bring it around in front and button.

TO DRAFT THE DIFFERENT SIZES

Take the measure of the child for the waist part and draft the same as the Child's Waist Draft. For the leg part, for each size larger add 1 inch to the length of the leg from waist line down.

Add ½ inch to the length of line Z-d and I-j.

LESSON XLV

To take the measures for Blouse —

Bust measure plus 2 inches
Neck measure
Waist measure plus 2 inches.
Armhole measure
Front Length to waist line.
Back Length to waist line.
Upper Front measure.
Front Length from neck to knee less 2 inches.
Back Length from neck to knee less 2 inches.
Back Width measure   Plus 1 inch.

Measures used for this draft

Bust	26	inches
Neck	9½	inches
Waist	25	inches
Armhole	13	inches
Front to waist	10	inches
Back to waist	9	inches
Upper Front	8½	inches
Back Width	9	inches
Front Length to knee	20	inches
Back Length to knee	19	inches

THE BLOUSE

1. Draw line A-B length of back to waist line.

2. From A measure the Under Arm measure. Mark this point C.

3. Continue line A-B above B, ½ inch. Mark this point **D**.

4. Square line at D with line A-D.

5   Measure from D on this line 1½ inches. Mark this point E.

6. Measure from C ½ of Bust measure. Mark this point F.

7. Measure from C on line C-F, ½ the Back Width measure. Mark this point G

8. At G square a line with line C-F.

9. From G measure on this line 1-3 the Armhole measure. Mark this point H.

10. Place point D on the chart at E and draw curve through H, continue ½ inch beyond H

11. Continue line G-H above H 1½ inches. Mark this point I.

12. At I square a line with line G-I.

13. From I on this line measure 2 inches. Mark this point J.

14. From G on line C-F measure ¼ the Armhole measure. Mark this point K.

15. Find a point half way between G and K. Mark this point L.

16. At K square a line with line C-F.

17. Measure from K on this line 2 inches. Mark this point M.

18. Place point G on the chart at the end of curve E-H and draw curve touching line G-H.

19. Place point K on the chart at the point where curve touches line G-H and draw curve through L.

20. Place point G at M and draw curve through L.

21. Place point F on the chart at M and draw curve through J.

22. Find the full length of curve E-H and measure this same distance from J on line I-J continued. Mark this point N.

23. Square a line with line C-F so that it will pass through N.

24. Measure on this line from line C-F the Upper Front measure less what is used in the back neck. Mark this point O.

25. Place point D on the chart at O and draw curve through J

26. Measure down from O ¼ of Neck measure. Mark this point P.

27. At P square a line with line O-P.

28. Measure from P on this line 1-6 of the Neck measure. Add ¼ inch. Mark this point Q

29. Place point J on the chart at Q and draw curve through O.

30. Draw line from Q through F.

31. Measure from Q on this line the Front Length measure to waist line Mark this point R.

32. At L square a line with line C-F.

33. Measure from L on this line the Under Arm measure. Mark this point S.

34. Measure 1 inch to the right and 1 inch to the left of S. Mark these points T and U.

35. Measure down from B the length of back to 2 inches above knee. Mark this point W.

36. Measure from Q the full length of front to 2 inches above knee. Mark this point V

37. Connect V and W with a straight line

38. Draw straight line from L through T and U and continue to line from V to W.

39. The line from L through U belongs to the back.

40. The line from L through T belongs to the front.

THE KNICKERBOCKERS

The Knickerbockers given are for a 2-year-old child.

Front of knickerbockers —

1. Draw line A-B 18½ inches long.

2. At B square a line with line A-B.

3. Measure on this line from B 8 inches. Mark this point C.

4. At C square a line with line B-C.

Boys' Russian Blouse.

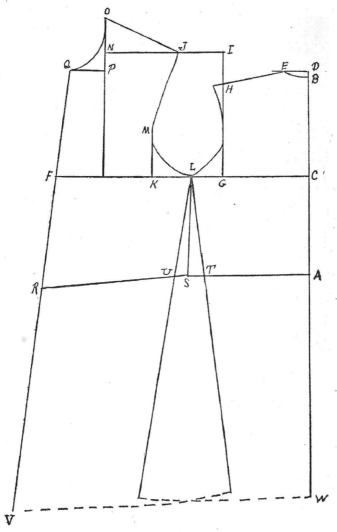

5. Measure on this line 16 inches. Mark this point D.

6. Square a line at D with line D-C and draw out to line A-B.

7. Measure from D on this line ¾ of an inch. Mark this point E.

8. Measure down from D on line C-D 7 inches. Mark this point F.

9. Place point C on the chart at F and draw curve to E.

10 Measure from line A-B on line from D 1½ inches. Mark this point G.

11. At G square a line with line D-G.

12. Measure from G on this line ¾ of an inch. Mark this point H.

13. Place point B on the chart at H and draw curve through E.

14. Measure from B on line A-B 8 inches. Mark this point I.

15. Square a line at I with line A-B.

16. Measure from I on this line 1¼ inches. Mark this point J.

17. Connect J and G with a straight line.

18. Measure from J on line J-G ¾ of an inch. Mark this point K.

19 Place point K on the chart at K and draw curve through I.

Back of knickerbockers —

1. At B square a line with line A-B.

2. Measure from B on this line 11½ inches. Mark this point L.

3 At L square a line with line B-L.

4 At A square a line with line A-B. Mark the point where this line meets line from L, M

5. From A on line A-M measure 5¼ inches. Mark this point N.

6. Find a point half way between B and I. Mark this point O.

7. Connect O and N with a straight line.

Boys' Knickerbockers.

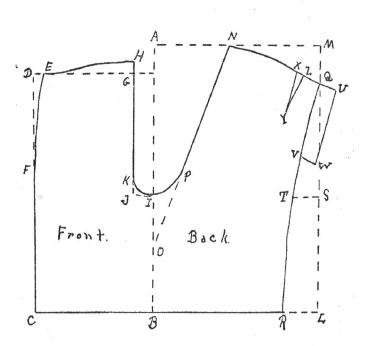

8. Place point K on the chart at I and hold chart so that J touches line O-N. Draw curve. Mark this point P.

9. Measure from M on line M-L 2½ inches. Mark this point Q.

10. Measure from B on line B-L 9 inches. Mark this point R.

11. Find a point half way between Q and L. Mark this point S.

12. At S square a line with line Q-L.

13. Measure from S on this line 2¼ inches. Mark this point T.

14 Place point C on the chart at R and draw curve to T.

15. Place point C on the chart at T and draw curve to Q

16. Continue line N-Q beyond Q 1¼ inches. Mark this point U.

17. Measure down from Q on curve Q-T 6 inches. Mark this point V.

18. Measure straight out from V 1¼ inches. Mark this point W.

19. Connect W and U with a straight line.

20. Measure from Q on curve Q-N 2 inches. Mark this point X.

21. Square a line at X and draw 3½ inches long. Mark this point Y.

22. Connect Y and X with a straight line.

23. Measure from X towards Q ½ inch. Mark this point Z.

24. Connect Z and Y with a straight line.

For every size larger, add 1 inch on lines B-C, B-L, A-M, D-G.

Add 1 inch on lines B-A, L-M, C-D.

Make the distance from B to I ½ inch more for each size.

LESSON XLVI

WE will teach you how to make the perfectly plain Russian Blouse, buttoned straight down the front This same blouse may have plaits down the front and back and it may be cut away in front at the neck and be finished with a large sailor collar. If you learn to make the plain garment you will be able to follow designs for more elaborate blouses. Lay line B-W on the lengthwise fold of the goods. Allow a large seam on the shoulder so if the blouse needs any fitting there will be goods enough to do it. Allow seams everywhere.

Cut two pieces like the front. Allow two inches on the bottom for hem. Sew in a French seam the under arm seams and shoulder seams, or the seams may be stitched and all turned one way and stitched again on the outside. Turn each front in about 1 inch for a hem, and after turning in the raw edge stitch as near the edge as possible. Turn the bottom up two inches, and after turning in the raw edge stitch the hem in.

Lap the right front over on the left 1 inch. Sew buttons on the right-hand side and work buttonholes on the left-hand side. Finish the neck with a round turn-over collar. (Cut the collar as directed for grown person) Use the child's full sleeve draft for the sleeves. Instead of gathering them in, plait them into the armhole and at the hand Begin at the middle of the sleeve and lay a small box plait Lay small side plaits on either side of this until the sleeve is the right size for the armhole and hand. Face the sleeve at the hand.

Place little straps made of the goods on the under arm seams, to hold a belt made of the goods or of leather

To make the knickerbockers — Cut out two pieces for the

fronts, and two for the backs. Lay line A-B each time on the straight of the goods lengthwise. Sew line B-I of the front to line B-I of the back. Sew line F-C of the front to line V-R of the back This forms the two separate legs Pin the two legs together at point I.

Sew line K-H of one front to line K-H of the other. Sew line I-N of one back to line I-N of the other Face the seam on each side of the front and put an under lap from I to K where the seam was not sewed. Turn in lap V-Q-U-W half way, so that it will form a hem and under lap. Fasten a pocket at line E-F on the front, or for very little children the pocket may be left out.

Sew in the dart X-Y-Z. Put a bias facing all about the top of the back, also the front, just the size of ½ the waist plus 2 inches for both the front and back, for the band must lap over 1 inch at each side where it fastens. Sew a button at E on each side, and work a buttonhole at Q on each side Work buttonholes all along the waist line to button on to the under waist. Put a hem in the bottom of each leg ½ inch wide and run elastic in, or gather the leg and put on a straight band, having a buckle sewed on the end. If this is done, seam B-I should be left open about 2 or 2½ inches from the bottom and both sides faced.

For a boy of 6 years or over the knickerbockers should fasten in the front instead of at the sides. In this case, where the pockets are put in at the sides, sew one side of the pocket to the front and the other to the back piece, having the seams on the inside. Turn each seam back and stitch again on the right side

Make the facing about the top all in one piece, opening at the front center seam. In cutting the pattern leave a projecting piece on the fronts at line H-K about 1½ inches wide. On the right side turn this piece back to form a hem, after having turned in the raw edge Take a straight piece of goods 3 inches wide and fold it lengthwise in the center. Turn the two raw edges in and place the piece just where the hem on the right

front will be stitched. This forms a fly for the buttonholes under the hem. Work buttonholes in this fly and catch it to the hem between the buttonholes Do not catch through to the outside. Line with a straight piece of the goods the projecting piece on the left front and allow it to project under the button-holes of the right side Place buttons on this piece to correspond with the buttonholes.

Put a pocket on each side of the back about $2\frac{1}{2}$ inches from the top, and about half way between the side and back seams. Make a pointed flap over each of these pockets, and put a button on the pocket and work a buttonhole in the corner of the flap.

LESSON XLVII

CHILD'S PAJAMA SUIT

To make the coat, draft the same as the child's waist draft. Add to the back of the neck $\frac{1}{4}$ inch, and $\frac{1}{2}$ inch at the waist line in the back Draw the middle back line through these two points. Leave out lines L-T and L-U.

Add 2 inches to the front at the middle line for lap, point W. Measure down from W 2 inches. Mark this point X. Place point F on the chart at X and allow curve F-J to touch curve O-Q

Add 4 inches to the bottom of the draft below waist line. In cutting out pattern allow seams everywhere. Turn the edge of the goods, about the neck and down the front, on the right side, and cover with a fancy braid or bias band of the goods Allow a hem $1\frac{1}{2}$ inches wide about the bottom. Lap the front so that line Q-R of one side comes on line Q-R of the other. Fasten down the front with buttons, or with fancy frog ornaments

The pajama part of the suit is drafted just like the knickerbockers, but the lines T-R, O-B, and F-C are extended below C-B-R enough to make them come to the ankles. This amount depends on the size of the child The dart is left out in the back, and gathered into the waist band. The front should be sewed to a waist made like the child's draft, but very loose about the waist and across the shoulders. The back is fastened to a band and buttoned to the waist For large boys the waist is not used The side seams are sewed up to the band and the pajamas are left open in front. A tape is fastened to each end of the band and tied in front. Place buttons and buttonholes down the front.

Boys' Pajama Suit.

LESSON XLVIII

CHILD'S DRAWERS

THE draft given is for a child of 5 years.

For every year in size add ¼ inch to front waist measure and ¼ inch to back waist measure, 1 inch to length of leg, and ¼ inch to width of leg on front and back.

The normal waist measures for children are as follows:

1 year old	20½ inches
2 years old	21 inches
3 years old	21½ inches
4 years old	22 inches
5 years old	22½ inches
6 years old	23 inches
7 years old	23 inches
8 years old	23½ inches
9 years old	23½ inches
10 years old	24 inches

1. Draw line A-B.

2. Find center between A and B. Mark this point C.

3. At C square a line with line A-B. Mark this point C-D.

4. From C on line C-D measure 1 inch   Mark this point E.

5. From C on line C-A measure 9 inches   Mark this point F.

6 From E on line C-D measure 15½ inches.   Mark this point G

7. At G square a line with line C-D.

8 Measure to the left of G 8¾ inches.   Mark this point H.

9. At H square a line with line G-H.

10. Measure from H on this line 3 inches.   Mark this point I.

11. Continue line G-H 4 inches.   Mark this point J.

12. At J square a line with line G-J.

13. Measure on this line from J 6½ inches.   Mark this point K.

14. Connect K and I with a straight line.

15. Place point F on the chart at I and draw curve through K.

16. Place point F on chart at I and draw through curve H.

17. Connect K and F with a straight line.

18. Find a point half way between F and K.   Mark this point L.

19. On this line measure ¾ of an inch from L.   Mark this point M.

20. Place point D on the chart at M and draw curve through K.

21. Place point D on the chart at M and draw curve through F.

This finishes the front of the drawers.

22. Measure from C on line C-B 7½ inches.   Mark this point N.

23. At N square a line with line C-B.

24. Measure from N on this line 1½ inches.   Mark this point O.

25. From G measure to the right 8¾ inches.   Mark this point P.

26. At P square a line with line G-P.

27. From P on this line measure 3 inches.   Mark this point Q.

28. Continue line G-P 4 inches.   Mark this point R.

29. At R square a line with line G-R.

30. From R measure on this line 6½ inches.   Mark this point S.

31. Connect S and Q with a straight line.

32. Place point F on the chart at Q and draw curve through S.

Childs' Drawers.

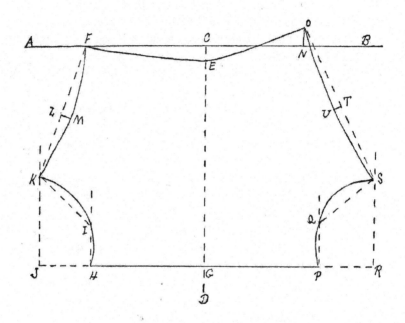

33. Place point F on the chart at Q and draw curve through P.

34. Connect S and O with a straight line.

35. Find a point half way between S and O. Mark this point T.

36. At T square a line with S-O.

37. Measure from T on this line ½ inch. Mark this point U.

38. Place point D on the chart at S and draw curve through U.

39. Place point C on the chart at U and draw curve through O.

This finishes the draft of the drawers.

In cutting patterns allow seams everywhere.

LESSON XLIX

FOR a little girl's dress the draft given may be used in a variety of ways

For the dress with the skirt gathered on at the waist line, use the draft just as it is. Cut a pattern by tracing off on another piece of paper, allowing seams everywhere, and about $1\frac{1}{4}$ inches down the back on each side for buttons and buttonholes Put all tucks in the goods before laying on the pattern. Any trimming like insertion of lace or embroidery may be laid on after the garment is cut, but this should be planned for before tucks are put in, so that the tucks will come just where they are wanted. After the waist is cut out, cut off lengths enough for the skirt to make it the desired fullness about the bottom. (This will depend on the size and age of the child.) From the breadth which is to be used for the front of the skirt, gore off about three inches, slanting out to the selvage. For the other breadths use the goods straight on both edges Allow a hem two or three inches wide. Gather this skirt to the waist at the waist line, placing more fullness in the back than in front. A belt of insertion of lace or embroidery may be used.

If the dress is to be MOTHER HUBBARD, use just the neck and shoulder part of the draft for a yoke and gather the skirt on to the yoke. Use the straight breadths, putting more fullness in the back than in front. If you wish to make a one-piece dress with box plaits down the front and back, trace the front and back on another piece of paper. Extend line Q-R straight down from R the length the skirt should be. Extend lines L-U and L-T down the same length but slant them out enough to make the skirt the desired fullness. A dress of this kind should not

have a very full skirt Extend line A-B down the same distance. Cut the pattern out, allowing all seams Lay box plaits in the goods lengthwise so that one will come in the middle front, and one about the middle of the shoulder line at each side In the back, one should be down the middle of the back and one each side about the middle of the shoulder line. These plaits should match on to each other at the shoulder. Cut an opening under each plait at the waist line and run a belt through. Either a leather belt or one of the goods may be used

Child's Blouse Waist. — To make the child's blouse waist, slant the middle back line out 1 inch at the waist line. Slant the front line out 1 inch at the waist line Draw straight line from L through U for the back under arm and draw a straight line from L through T for the under arm of the front. Add $2\frac{1}{2}$ inches to the bottom of the waist. Put a narrow hem in the bottom aud run an elastic in

Little Girl's Under Clothing. — For the little girl's under waist this same draft may be used. Face the bottom with a bias facing about $1\frac{1}{2}$ inches wide and the armholes with a bias facing 1 inch wide. Make a hem down each side of the back and work buttonholes and sew on buttons Place the buttonholes on the right hand side. Sew buttons about the bottom to button the waist on.

Little Girl's Skirt. — Make the skirt straight, and not quite as full as the dress skirt. Place a hem in the bottom about $1\frac{1}{2}$ inches wide and a straight band at the waist line about $1\frac{1}{4}$ inches wide Leave the skirt open about 7 or 8 inches down the back and hem the left side with a hem $\frac{3}{4}$ inch wide and the right side with a narrow hem. Lap the wide hem over on the narrow one at the bottom and stitch across the bottom to keep it from tearing down Work buttonholes in the waist band to match the buttons on the waist If desired the skirt may be sewed to the waist, but this is not desirable, as one often wishes to change one of the garments and not the other.

Child's Drawers. — Cut two pieces like the draft. Sew curve

K-I-H to curve S-Q-P. Sew line F-M-K of one piece to the same line of the other   Slash both pieces down from E about 6 inches. Face this slash with a continuous facing. Leave the front side out for an under lap and turn the other back. Gather the waist line of the back to a straight band 2 inches longer than ½ the waist measure and the back to a straight band the same length. This band should be about 1½ inches wide when finished   Sew a button to each end of the front band and work a buttonhole in each end of the back band. Work buttonholes in the middle at the back and front to button on the waist.

Child's Night-gown. — Use the child's waist draft. For a perfectly plain gown use the draft as it is, leaving out lines L-U and L-T. Draw lines slanting out from L to make the desired fullness about the bottom, according to the size of the child. Cut both the back and front on a fold of the goods lengthwise. Cut the front open on the center front line to about 4 or 5 inches below the waist line   Hem the left side of the opening with a very narrow hem and the right side with an inch-wide hem. Lay the right side over on the left and stitch across the bottom. Face the neck with a bias facing and sew a little edge to it   Trim the sleeves at the hand the same way. Use the full sleeve draft. Put a hem in the bottom about 1½ inches wide   The gown may be made full about the neck if desired.   For this allow 2 inches on the back and 3 on the front. Gather about the neck and then face as in the plain gown.

Blouse Waist.

LESSON L

The Pinning Blanket. — For the skirt.

1. Draw line A-B 25 inches long.
2. At A, square a line with line A-B
3. Draw 5 inches long   Mark this point C.
4 Measure up from C ½ inch   Mark this point D.
5. Place point D on the chart at A and draw curve through D.
6. At B square a line with line A-B
7. Measure from B on this line 14 inches   Mark this point E.
8 Connect D and E with a straight line.
9 Measure from D on line D-E the same distance as A to B. Mark this point F. Connect B and F with a slightly curved line.
10 Draw line G-H 25 inches long.
11 At G square a line with line G-H.
12. Measure from G 7½ inches   Mark this point I
13. Measure up from I 1½ inches   Mark this point J.
14 At H square a line with line G-H and draw 16½ inches long   Mark this point K.
15. Connect J and K with a straight line
16 Measure down from J the same distance as from G to H. Mark this point L
17 Connect L and H with a curved line.
18. Place point D on the chart at G and draw curve to J.

•

THE WAIST·

19. Draw line M-N 5 inches long.

20. At M square a line with line M-N and draw 13 inches long. Mark this point O

21. Measure up from O, ½ inch. Mark this point P

22. Measure from M on line M-O, 7½ inches. Mark this point Q

23. Place point C on the chart at P and draw curve through Q

24. At N square a line with line M-N and draw 13 inches long. Mark this point R

25. Measure down from R, ½ inch   Mark this point S.

26 Measure from N, 3 inches. Mark this point T.

27 Place point D on the chart at S and draw curve through T.

28 Measure to the left of Q, 3 inches   Mark this point U.

29 At Q square a line with line O-Q and draw 5 inches long. Mark this point V.

30. Place point F on the chart at U and draw curve to V

31. Continue line Q-V above V 1½ inches.   Mark this point W.

32. At W square a line with line Q-W.   Draw 1½ inches long. Mark this point X

33. Measure to the left of U, 2 inches. Mark this point Y.

34. Place point F on the chart at Y and draw curve through X

35. Find a point half way between U and Q.   Mark this point Z.

36 With Z as a center and Z-U as a radius connect U and Q with a curve.

The pinning blanket is made of white flannel

Cut two pieces for the fronts and two for the backs   Join the two backs at line J-L.   Join line G-H to line D-F.   These seams should be pressed open and cat-stitched on the right side with white silk.

Put a hem 1½ inches wide down the fronts and about the bottom.   Baste the hem in and cat-stitch it on the right side with silk, catching through so as to fasten the hem in   Cut the waist with line M-N on a fold of the goods   Cut two pieces, as the waist is made double   Stitch the two pieces together all about the top and ends   Turn and baste the edges together so as to make a nice smooth edge.   Stitch again all around, and turn in the two lower edges.   Slip the top edge of the skirt part in between these edges, having point J come at N.   Stitch across on the machine on the right side.   Work a buttonhole in the end of the shoulder strap, and place buttons as indicated on draft.

THE INFANT'S SKIRT

The waist portion is made almost like the waist of the pinning blanket.   In this waist line N-R is used for the bottom and line M-O for the top.   Measure out to the left of N ½ inch.   Place point D on the chart at N and draw curve through M.   This is the front line of the skirt waist.   This part was used in the back for the pinning blanket   There must be a seam in this waist as it is a curve.   Make the waist just as you did the other except that it will be made of fine muslin.

Make the skirt portion straight of the goods, making each breadth 26 inches long   The skirt should measure 1½ yards about the bottom.   Put a hem in the bottom 1¼ inches wide, and open the skirt down the back 4 inches.   Sew to the waist as in the other case, placing the gathers between the two parts of the waist.   Put a hem ¾ of an inch down both sides of the back, and down the skirt opening.   Lap at the bottom as directed for other garments.

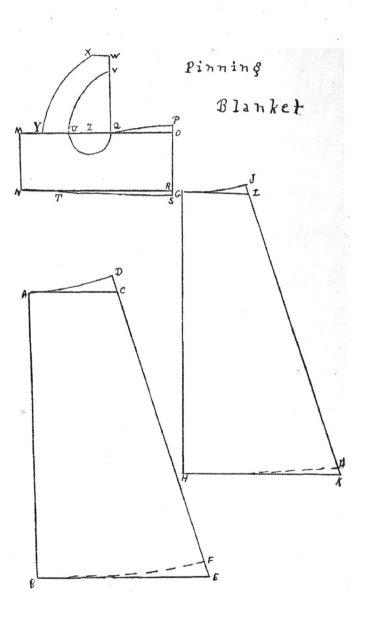

Pinning

Blanket

THE INFANT'S SLIP OR NIGHT-GOWN

Back of gown —

1. Draw line A-B 36 inches long.
2. At A, square a line with line A-B
3. From A measure on this line 4¾ inches. Mark this point C.
4. Measure up from A ¼ inch   Mark this point D.
5. Measure to the right of A 1¾ inches. Mark this point E.
6. At E, square a line with line A-C.
7. Measure from E on this line ¾ inch   Mark this point F.
8. Place point K on the chart at F, and draw curve to D.
9. Connect F and C with a straight line.
10. Measure down from A on line A-B 3 inches. Mark this point G.
11. At G square a line with line A-B.
12. Measure from G on this line 6 inches   Mark this point H.
13. Measure to the left of H ¾ inch. Mark this point I.
14 Place point J on the chart at C and draw curve to I. Continue curve to H.
15 Square a line at B, with line A-B.
16. Measure from B on this line 17 inches   Mark this point J.
17 Connect H and J with a straight line
18. Measure from H on line H-J 32 inches. Mark this point K.
19 Connect B and K with a slight curve.

Front of gown —

1. Draw line A-B 36 inches long.
2. At A square a line with line A-B.
3. Measure from A on this line 6½ inches. Mark this point C.
4. At C square a line with line A-C.

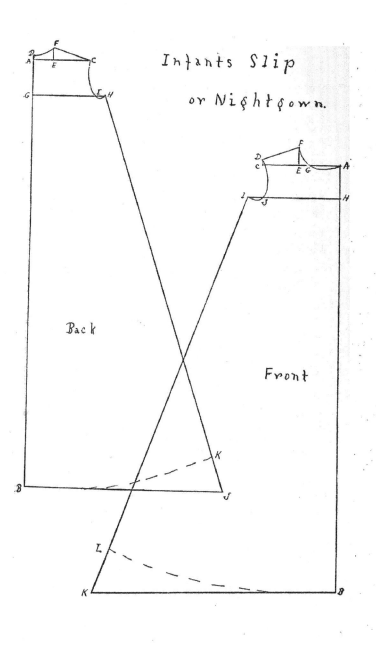

Infants Slip or Nightgown.

5 Measure from C on this line, ½ inch. Mark this point D.

6. Measure to the right of C, 3 inches. Mark this point E.

7. At E square a line with line A-C.

8 Measure from E on this line, 1½ inches. Mark this point F.

9 Connect F and D with a straight line.

10. Measure to the right of D, 1 inch. Mark this point G.

11. Place point K on the chart at G and draw curve through F.

12. Measure down from A on line A-B, 2½ inches. Mark this point H.

13. At H square a line with line A-B.

14. Measure from H on this line, 7¾ inches. Mark this point I

15. Measure to the right of I, 1½ inches. Mark this point J.

16. Place point J on the chart at D and draw curve to J.

17. Place point K on the chart at J and draw curve to I.

18. At B square a line with line A-B

19. Measure from B on this line, 21 inches   Mark this point K.

20. Connect K and I with a straight line

21. Measure from I on this line, 32 inches   Point L.

22. Connect L and I with a slight curve.

Infant's sleeve —

1. Draw line A-B 5½ inches long.

2. At B square a line with line A-B.

3. Measure from B on this line 10 inches   Mark this point C.

4. Measure from B ½ inch.   Mark this point D.

5. Place point D on the chart at D and draw curve through A.

6. Find a point half way between D and C.   Mark this point E.

Infants Sleeve.

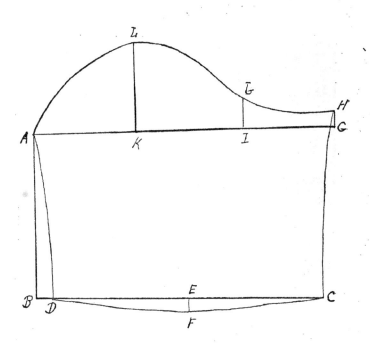

7. Square a line at E with line D-C.

8. From E on this line, measure ½ inch   Mark this point F.

9 Place point D on the chart at F and draw curve through D.

10 Place point D on the chart at F and draw curve through C.

11. At A square a line with line A-B.

12. Measure from A on this line 10½ inches. Mark this point G.

13. At G square a line with line A-G.

14. Measure from G on this line ½ inch. Mark this point H.

15 Place point D on the chart at C and draw curve through H.

16. Measure to the left of G 3 inches. Mark this point I.

17 At I, square a line with line A-G. ·

18. Measure from I on this line, 1 inch   Point J.

19. Place point F on the chart at H and draw curve through J.

20. Find a point half way between A and I. Mark this point K

21. At K square a line with line A-G.

22. Measure on this line from K 3 inches. Mark this point L.

23. Place point N on the chart at L and draw curve through A.

24. Place point N on the chart at L and draw curve through J.

HOW TO MAKE THE SLIP OR NIGHT-GOWN

Cut the middle back and middle front lines on the lengthwise fold of the goods   Sew up the under arm seams in a very narrow French seam. Put a hem in the bottom, 1 inch wide for the night-gown, and run a tape in for a draw string. Sew the shoulders in a narrow French seam. Slash the front down 14 inches and hem as in the child's gown. Turn the neck down a small seam and cover with finishing braid   Sew to the edge of this a narrow lace edge. Gather the sleeves at the hand and finish with the finishing braid and edge

For the slip put a three inch hem in the bottom, and do not use the draw string   Sew in the sleeve and the garment is finished.

FOR THE INFANT'S DRESS

Trace off a yoke of any desired shape, using the draft for the slip. Add 3 inches to the center front and 3 inches to the center back for gathers   Make the dress when finished 36 inches long; it may have a wide hem in the bottom or a ruffle 3 inches wide on the bottom   The ruffle should be 1½ the width of the skirt in fullness. The dress may be as fancy as you wish, using tucks and lace or embroidery. Do not use ruffles about the neck or sleeves. The skirt of the dress should measure about 2 3-8 yards about the bottom. Use the sleeve draft given.

LESSON LI

THERE are three ways in which you can turn your knowledge into money. Draft patterns for others, go out by the day to sew, or open an establishment of your own   If you do the latter you can easily combine the second with it.

To open an establishment of your own, you may set aside certain rooms in your own home for your work, or you may open rooms in some convenient place in the down town district   In one way the latter is best. You can get completely away from your work when working hours are over. The expense, however, is greater.

For your work you should have three rooms. A waiting-room, a fitting-room, and a workroom.   The first should be small but comfortable, and in good taste   The second may be small, but should have a good light and, if possible, a mirror coming nearly to the floor. The workroom should be light, warm and large. In this room should be kept all working utensils. You should have in this room a gas plate or small stove for heating flat-irons. A good plan is to tack a large piece of muslin on the wall in this room to pin patterns on. This will be found better than to fold them   Keep all patterns of regular patrons   If possible have a closet off of this room to hang your finished and partly finished work in. Have two or three wooden boxes (cigar boxes) to put all the little utensils in, such as pencils, tracing-wheels, tracing-chalk, etc. Always keep your chart where it will not get broken NEVER SHOW THE GOWNS YOU MAKE TO ANY ONE BUT THE PERSON FOR WHOM THEY ARE MADE. It is not professional   You will lose your patrons if you do. When you are ready to open your establishment, send to all your friends your calling-card, upon which you have neatly written the word DRESSMAKING.

Keep your sewing-room as orderly as possible. If you need help, train a person to each part of the business. Give one sleeves, one skirts, one waists, etc.

You must keep a book for your accounts, and put in it everything you furnish for your patrons, and the cost of each article. Do not purchase any expensive material for a customer without having first had them make a deposit with you of at least $\frac{1}{2}$ the cost of the article. Send a bill with every piece of work you send out. If this is not paid in one month send another bill. Keep on sending them each month until paid   In figuring the cost of a gown be sure to get in every item, and be sure not to forget to add a profit if you are to furnish the material   Go to your dry goods merchant the first thing and get a dressmaker's discount. Never give a customer this discount. if you do the merchant will take it from you.

THE END

CPSIA information can be obtained
at www.ICGtesting.com
Printed in the USA
BVOW06*0214050617

486043BV00005B/22/P